IN SEARCH OF HIROSHI

A JAPANESE AMERICAN ODYSSEY

KAYA PRESS

LOS ANGELES
NEW YORK

Published by Kaya Press // kaya.com
Distributed by D.A.P./Distributed Art Publishers // artbook.com (800) 388-BOOK
ISBN: 9781885030825
Library of Congress Control Number: 2023952333
Cover design by Spoon & Fork (spoonandforkstudio.com)
Cover art by Keisho Okayama, *Two Heads/Dark Center*, 1994 (keishookayama.com)

This book was made possible by support from the USC Dana and David Dornsife College of Arts, Letters, and Sciences; the USC Department of American Studies and Ethnicity; Stephen CuUnjieng; and the Choi Chang Soo Foundation.
　Additional funding was provided by generous contributions from: Fuad Ahmad, Tanzila Ahmed, Kamil Ahsan, Jasmine Ako, Christine Alberto, Hari Alluri, Stine An, Akhila Ananth, Tiffany Babb, Manibha Banerjee, Tom and Lily So Beischer, Terry Bequette, Piyali Bhattacharya, Roddy Bogawa, Paul Bonnell, Thi Bui, Hung Bui, Cari Campbell, Nate Cavalieri, Susan Chan, Sonali Chanchani, Jade Chang, Wah-Ming Chang, Alexander Chee, Anelise Chen, Anita Chen, Jean Chen, Lisa Chen, Leland Cheuk, Floyd Cheung, Amy Chin, Elaine Cho, Jayne Choi, Judy Choi, Jennifer Chou, Seo-Young Chu, Elizabeth Clements, Tuyet Cong Ton Nu, Timothy Daley, Matthew Dalto, Kavita Das, Lawrence-Minh Bùi Davis, Steven Doi, Susannah Donahue, Daniel Dyer, Irving Eng, Jessica Eng, Fan Fan, Matthew Fargo, Peter Feng, Sia Figiel, Sesshu Foster, Christopher Fox, Sylvana Freyberg, Naomi Fukuchi, Kelsey Grashoff, Anthony Hale, KA Hashimoto, Jean Ho, Skye Hodges, Ann Holler, Heidi Hong, Huy Hong, Abeer Hoque, Jonathan Hugo, Jimmy Hwang, Ashaki Jackson, Jayson Joseph, Theresa Kang, Mia Kang, Lisa Kang, Andrew Kebo, Vandana Khanna, Bizhan Khodabandeh, Swati Khurana, Ian Kim, Helen Kim Lee, Gwendolyn Knight, Sabrina Ko, Robin Koda, Karen Koh, Juliana Koo, Sun Hee Koo, Eileen Kurahashi, Paul Lai, Jenny Lam, Iris Law, Samantha Le, Catherine Lee, Hyunjung Lee, Whakyung Lee in memory of Sonya Choi Lee, Winona Leon, Andrew Leong, Edan Lepucki, Claire Light, Janine Lim, Edward Lin, Jennifer Liou, Carleen Liu, Mimi Lok, Leza Lowitz, Pauline Lu, Abir Majumdar, Jason McCall, Sally McWilliams, Rajiv Mohabir, Faisal Mohyuddin, Russell Morse, Samhita Mukhopadhyay, Nayomi Munaweera, Adam Muto, Wendy Lou Nakao, Jean Young Naylor, Dominique Nguyen, Kathy Nguyen, Kim Nguyen, Vinh Nguyen, Viet Thanh Nguyen, Sandra Noel, Yun and Minkyung Oh, Gene & Sabine Oishi, Chez Bryan Ong, Eric Ong, Tiffany Ong, Camille Patrao, Perlita Payne, Leena Pendharker, Thuy Phan, Eming Piansay, Cheryline Prestolino, James Pumarada, Zhiyao Qiu, Jhani Randhawa, Amarnath Ravva, Sam Robertson, Brendan Ryan, Jonathan Sands, Chaitali Sen, Prageeta Sharma, Andrew Shih, Paul H. Smith, Roch Smith, Luisa Smith, Nancy Starbuck, Rachana Sukhadia, Robin Sukhkadia, Rajen Sukhadia, Kelly Sutherland, Willie Tan, Zhen Teng, Isabella Tilley, Wendy Tokuda, Frederick Tran, Monique Truong, Kosiso Ugwueze, Patricia Wakida, Monona Wali, Kelli Washington, Aviva Weiner, Heather Werber, Rachel Will, Duncan Williams, William Wong, Koon Woon, Amelia Wu & Sachin Adarkar, Andrea Wu, Anita Wu & James Spicer, Ann Yamamoto, Jihfang Yang, Nancy Yap, Max Yeh, Stan Yogi, Shinae Yoon, Mikoto Yoshida, and many others.
　Additional support for Kaya Press is provided by the National Endowment for the Arts; the Los Angeles County Board of Supervisors through the Los Angeles County Arts Commission; the Community of Literary Magazines and Presses and the Literary Arts Emergency Fund; and the City of Los Angeles Department of Cultural Affairs.
　Finally, special thanks to Austin Nguyen, Paul Liu, and Kaitlin Hsu for their work on this book.

IN SEARCH OF HIROSHI

A JAPANESE AMERICAN ODYSSEY

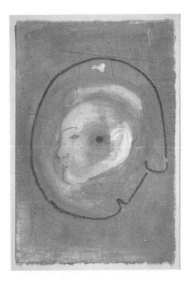

GENE OISHI

FOR SABINE

PREFACE

It has been more than three decades since *In Search of Hiroshi* was published by the Charles E. Tuttle Company. Much has changed since then, both in myself and within our country. I am no longer a young man in search of himself, and it is our country which, at this writing, seems to be in search of its soul. Even so, I am deeply gratified that Kaya Press, which published my novel, *Fox Drum Bebop*, has found my memoir worthy of republication.

To this new edition, I have added an Epilogue to account for the changes that have taken place since the original publication. The French have a saying, plus ça change, plus c'est la même chose, which suggests that even when it appears outwardly that great changes have taken place, everything actually remains the same. The resurgence of racial prejudices and animosities in the United States might support this point of view, but my memoir is not about the state of our country, but about how I view my place in it. From this personal perspective, much has changed, and Hiroshi in meaning and context is no longer the same.

Hiroshi was based on my childhood experience of being one

of the 110,000 Japanese Americans living on the West Coast of the United States arrested and put in concentration camps at the start of World War II and how that experience impacted my life. I considered changing the point of view by updating the narrative voice to take into account my dismay at the recent wave of racism and xenophobia that have become increasingly prevalent. But the book is a memoir that reflects my experiences and the cultural and political environment of the trauma I experienced in childhood and its enduring effects. It is a book written by one who had not yet found answers to questions about his past. As the title implies, it is a search, not an autobiography written in the fullness of time.

In the postwar years, I shrugged off the mass incarceration as one of those unfortunate events that will occur in war. Its effects on us, I thought, were mainly economic. Before the war, my father had farmed vast acres of land in California's Santa Maria Valley, employing hundreds of field workers. When Japanese naval forces attacked the U.S. naval base at Pearl Harbor on December 7, 1941, he was one of the many other leaders of Japanese communities on the West Coast of the United States arrested by FBI agents that very night. The rest of us were allowed to remain in our homes for a few months until camps were built in wilderness areas in the interior of the country. Japanese communities along the West Coast of the United States were emptied; farmers and businesses were ruined. When we returned to our home after the war, my parents had to join labor gangs like those my father had employed before the war. Some of the work was done while stooping, but my parents were too old for that and had to shuffle along on their knees. Strangely, it was only years later, when I was married with children of my own, that I fully understood the humiliation my parents had endured and the courage with which they faced and survived their impoverishment.

Understanding the war and its aftermath came slowly and in unexpected ways. One such moment was reading of soldiers returning from Afghanistan and Iraq who were diagnosed with

PTSD and unable to make clear a clear connection between their problems and the trauma of combat. I was reminded of what used to be called "battle fatigue," except that the new designation stressed psychic injuries showing up after the soldiers have come home where they were presumably safe. What interested me is that victims of PTSD were sometimes unable to make a clear connection between their problems and the trauma of combat. My guess is that some of these soldiers blamed themselves for whatever it was that troubled them. Some resorted to suicide, a solution I too have contemplated in the past.

I do not compare myself to soldiers returning from the horrors of war, except that in some cases they seemed to be in a state of denial. I insisted for years that I was not seriously affected by my wartime experience. My family and I were taken from our home and imprisoned in a place surrounded by barbed wire and guarded by soldiers armed with rifles with fixed bayonets and machine guns. My father had lost everything he had worked to build over four decades in America. I told myself that such things happen in war, and it took me years to get past the protective cloak I had wrapped around myself.

Long after the war, a white friend asked me to describe the camps and how we were treated. I told him the guards would strip us naked, tie us spread-eagled to stakes in the desert, and pour honey over us so that ants would come and feed on us. My friend laughed and protested my black humor. "Hey," I said, clawing at my shirt, "you want to see the scars?" More than two decades after the imprisonment, I still had difficulty talking about it. I did not dare look too deeply into myself to find out how I really felt about the experience, but my joke described my condition more accurately than I realized at the time. I was eaten alive in the desert, not by ants but by doubts—doubts about myself, my parents, and my cultural identity. I was assailed by notions that there was something wrong with me, or with my parents, or with Japanese generally.

Hiroshi had started out as a novel because I thought fiction was a better vehicle for exploring facets of my life that were based on childhood memories. But fiction, like music, touches on deep wells of feelings hidden from the conscious mind. I found myself unable to manipulate my memories in such a way as to produce the emotional impact, great or subtle, that fiction requires. When I once had a character in my story say, "I am Japanese," I inexplicably broke into tears and could not continue. I remained, for years, in this emotional writer's block.

I began to get a better understanding of the emotional baggage I was carrying when, in the early 1980s, *National Geographic* asked me to write an article about the postwar success of Japanese Americans. I traveled the country interviewing scores of Japanese, including first generation immigrants, their children, and their grandchildren. Hearing their stories and residual feelings about their wartime experience took me out of my self-imposed isolation and I ended up writing not a happy success story about the "model minority," but one of anguish, pain and unresolved fears and anger. *National Geographic* rejected it, but *The New York Times Magazine* published an abridged version headlined "The Anxiety of Being Japanese American."

The interviews I conducted for the article made me realize that my childhood trauma that I had long suppressed was real and shared by other Japanese Americans throughout the country. That the *New York Times Magazine* would print my first-person account of my wartime experiences and their aftereffects gave me the incentive to write this book.

We are all affected by world events that are beyond our control but nevertheless profoundly shape and direct our lives. For me, like for millions of others, it was World War II. The war impacted Japanese Americans in a unique way that was not only financially ruinous, but also shook and threatened our very identity. I eventually gave a name to that still shaky sense of self, a Japanese American boy named Hiroshi to serve as my fictional surrogate.

He became my lifeboat. To survive emotionally, I needed to find Hiroshi who defined my place in this world. Socrates seemed on to something when he said that an unexamined life is not worth living. I found that my years of denial of my childhood trauma and my failure to examine and confront the damage it did to me, my family and Japanese Americans generally had been filled with confusion and avoidable pain. The search for Hiroshi was a search for my own identity and to understand and to rid myself of this crippling burden I've been carrying through most of my life. To be sure, the woes of this world continue and I am like most of humanity, a leaf blown hither and yon by the wind. But my understanding of who and what I am is now with me and under my command.

Gene Oishi & his father in Long Beach in 1946

1

I was born in 1933 in Guadalupe, California, a small farming community about 200 miles up the coast from Los Angeles. Guadalupe is not a town people drive through on their way to somewhere else; it is not on a road that goes to any place important. Guadalupe is its own justification. The county road coming into town becomes Main Street when it hits a clutter of small stores. The street bends about a third of the way up and continues for another block or two before it recedes into the countryside. There are some small residential sections, but just about all the businesses are in this crook in the road that we used to call "downtown."

When I was growing up, Guadalupe was like a Japanese colony. We had our own restaurants, grocery stores, fish market, pool halls, gambling houses, barber, beauty shop, doctor, dentist, Buddhist church, Japanese school and classical dance teacher. Once a week we went to the hall of the Seinen-Dan, the young men's association, to see Japanese movies. There were newsreels that showed scenes from Japan and sometimes from Manchuria and China. Those movies blend in my memory with faded family photographs taken in Japan and in Guadalupe during the early days. Other images come from stories my father told about his childhood in Japan and about his first years in America and from Japanese tales my mother read to me. There were magazines from Japan that had drawings of battlefields lined with barbed wire and trenches filled with huddled soldiers smoking cigarettes and writing letters. As a child, my favorite song was about a Japanese soldier in Manchuria writing a letter home. "This is a place countless hundreds of ri from the homeland," the song began. When I asked why Japanese soldiers were in Manchuria, my mother said that Japan was a small country and needed more room for its people.

And now, Manchuria, a place I have never seen, sticks in my memory. Like Guadalupe, it is a state of mind, of not belonging, of distance from the homeland, of not being able to understand and of explanations that do not convince. Despite all the patriotic sentiment, there was a forlorn note in that song of the Japanese soldier. It seemed that he did not feel he belonged in Manchuria and he wanted to go home. There have been many times in my life when I felt as he did. I did not belong and I wanted to go home. But where was that? When I last visited Guadalupe in 1983, I could no longer think of it as my hometown. There were hardly any Japanese left and nearly all the businesses were now run by Mexicans and whites. When I was a child, there was a thriving Japanese community where everybody knew everybody else, a place where I belonged, was accepted and safe. That was gone and the only home I had left was the one in my head – a home without substance, made only of memories.

My father, too, did not feel he belonged. He had come to America in 1903 at the age of nineteen, thinking he would spend only a few years in the country, just long enough to make a lot of money so he could return to Japan a wealthy man. He stayed longer than he had intended. After he was here for seven years, he wrote to his father in Japan and asked him to find him a wife. Shortly thereafter, a 17-year-old orphan girl came from Japan to marry him. When their oldest daughter Yoshiko was six and their son Nimashi five, they took them to Japan to live with relatives and to be educated in Japanese schools. They had a third child at the time, a three-year-old daughter named Hiroko, and later, five more children came. I was the last. We were kept in America and educated in American schools, perhaps because the prospect of returning to Japan was getting increasingly remote.

Yoshiko came back to Guadalupe when she was eighteen and a marriage was arranged for her to a young Japanese dentist in Los Angeles. "It was such a good opportunity for her," my mother explained to me when I questioned her about it as an adult. "To be married to a dentist. She would be comfortable for the rest of her life." Nimashi came back, too, but he did not get along with Papa, so he returned to Japan to continue his schooling. Two years later, Nimashi was ordered back to Guadalupe because Papa feared that if he stayed in Japan he would be drafted into the Japanese Army, which was fighting in China. In their old age, my parents regretted deeply their decision to send Yoshiko and Nimashi to Japan, for the damaged familial bonds were never completely restored. Nimashi, whom we younger children addressed respectfully as "Ni-san," or older brother, seemed isolated not only from his parents but from his brothers and sisters as well. He was not like the rest of us. His younger siblings, who spoke English among themselves, spoke Japanese to him just as they did with their parents. As the youngest and still in preschool, I also spoke only Japanese, so I may have been the only one of his siblings to establish a close relationship with him.

I thought of Hiroko as our oldest sister; Yoshiko was already married and living in Los Angeles by the time I was born. Yoshiro, the second son, was Papa's favorite because, Papa said, he was so mentally alert and diligent. The third son, Goro, was a very quiet and shy boy, who idolized his older brother. "Yosh is going to be a great man someday," Goro often said. The fourth son, Rokuro, died of encephalitis when he was six, so I never knew him. Hoshiko, the youngest girl, was supposed to be the last child, and because she was thought to be the baby of the family, everybody called her by a diminutive, "Ho-chan." Seven years after she was born, however, I came along as something of a surprise.

My parents named me Yoshitaka, written with two Chinese characters, one standing for goodness and the other for filial piety. They also gave me an American name, although they had not done that with any of their other children. Thirty years had passed since my father came to America, and his resolve to return to Japan had weakened. But it was not dead and it troubled him, as it did my mother, that their younger children were becoming increasingly American, singing American songs, chattering among themselves in English, listening to American radio shows and reading American books and magazines. Like most Japanese children in Guadalupe, we went to learn Japanese at the Buddhist church, where classes were held every day after regular school was over. Although we did learn the rudiments of reading and writing Japanese, it ceased to be our mother tongue after a time. American influences were too strong. Our Japanese was corrupted and we often spoke to our parents in a mixture of English and Japanese. Because of our deficiencies in language, my parents worried about what would become of us when we returned to Japan—something none of us children thought would ever happen.

My father, however, could not give up his dream of returning one day to Japan. So, nothing he did in America had any permanence. The house he built for his family was nothing more than temporary quarters tacked onto the rear of a general store. It was hastily constructed out of cheap pine, and the roof was topped with corrugated metal. At the time I was born, the house was only two years old, but I remember it as old and dilapidated. Because the house was built on sloping ground, most of it was on a stilt-like foundation, which formed an above-ground basement, or the "downcellar," as we called it. There were rats that gnawed holes through the floor, and pieces of tin cut out of soup cans were nailed over them. Winds buffeted the house, making it sway and creak, and on a wintry night, you could feel the cold blast coming through the cracks in the wall. The roof frequently rusted through, and until it was repaired, my mother would place pots, pans, and buckets around to catch the drips when it rained. As a child I would not have experienced these things on my own as something out of the ordinary, but my mother was always complaining about them.

My mother was already forty years old when I was born. She was a plump woman, a little over five feet tall, with long, jet-black hair which she kept tied in a bun at the back of her head. "This house," she would say. "How can anyone keep a house like this clean? The dust comes right up through the floor. There is no sense in cleaning a house like this. It is just as dirty again the next day." Still, she was always sweeping, vacuuming, and mopping, and I wondered why she bothered if everything she said was true. When I got sick, which was often, she would say, "This house. How can anyone raise healthy children in a house like this? The wind comes right through the walls. It is always cold and drafty."

My mother, it seemed to me, was always angry at my father, but she did not dare confront him, for he was a large man with a volcanic temper. The most dangerous time was before dinner if he was in a bad mood. Once, he threw his soup bowl, soup and all, into the garbage can because the main dish was too slow in coming. I was amazed at the accuracy of his throw and afraid that he would throw something next at my mother, who scurried about saying through gritted teeth, "Hai, hai. Right away, right away." Actually, my father was not in the habit of striking his wife or children. When he was in one of his fits of temper, he would threaten us with banishment. "Get out!" he would shout. "Get out of this house." Being thrown out of the house could mean being thrown out of the family. In Japan, in extreme cases, the name of the offending child would be erased from the family register, and he or she would cease to exist as far as the family was concerned.

In recent years, I have wondered why my father was so quick to threaten his children with punishment as drastic as that when he must have felt like an exile himself. Early in his marriage he even ordered his young wife and infant daughter out of the house for an offense so minor that my mother, when she spoke about it years later, could not remember what it was. I was already an adult when she first told me. She spoke with some bitterness about how she had to swallow her pride and go back and ask her husband's forgiveness. "Where was I to go with a baby in a strange country?" At the time, she was eighteen years old and had been in America less than two years. When my father died, my mother sat in a chair, absorbed in her thoughts, saying, "There were times when I said, 'When you die, I will not cry for you,' but here I am crying after all."

With me, the baby of the family, the threat was not as abstract as banishment. My father would pick me up and threaten to throw me bodily out of the house. My mother would come running and there would be a tugging match at the door with my mother pulling me back into the house by my legs while my father pointed my head out the door. My father would eventually give in, but not before I was thoroughly terrorized. Even more frightening to me was the cellar. I was afraid of it because of the rats, but a special place of terror for me was the hole that led to the crawlspace under the storefront. It was dark and dank in there, the soil was black, sinister, and evil. In my imagination, all forms of horrible, gruesome creatures resided in its depths—huge, slimy, crawly things that would devour you slowly, even lovingly. My father could not have known that for me, that was a place of horror, but he knew I was afraid of it. Once, he threatened to lock me in that hole. My mother was there tugging at my legs as I struggled helplessly against my father's grip, my head thrust in that black void. I was so paralyzed with fear that I could not make a sound. It was only after my mother carried me upstairs and held and rocked me in her arms that the tears began to flow and I could sob audibly.

2

My father died in 1965 at the age of 81. I was 32 at the time, married and working as a reporter for *The Baltimore Sun*. The flight back to California was a journey back in time. Although I was going to San Pedro where my family then lived, in my mind I was returning to Guadalupe, to a childhood that had been dominated by my father. I wondered about this man whose death I was being called back to mourn.

The funeral was held at the Nishi Hongwanji, one of the main Buddhist temples in Los Angeles. Seven priests in purple and gold brocade stood before the coffin chanting the Sutra while another sounded the prayer gong. The sanctuary was filled with large floral arrangements on tall easels that were massed on both sides of the coffin and strung out along the walls. The scent of flowers was almost overpowering, but the burning incense cut through it, creating that sweet, pungent mixture of fragrances that I recalled from childhood. It was the most elaborate funeral I had ever seen, and my brother Yoshiro kept saying, "Papa would have been happy." He and the others were pleased that so many of the surviving prewar "big shots"—former farmers mainly—were there. These old men in ill-fitting suits, who shuffled and bowed, who mixed me up with one of my brothers, had held the power in the world in which I lived as a child. Now, I saw them as powerless immigrants, castaways from their homeland. Their power was nothing in the white world that surrounded us. Yet they had once seemed to me to be infinitely powerful, and the most powerful of all now lay serenely in a coffin. The undertakers had done a good job, stuffing his mouth with cotton to fill out his cheeks. His face was smooth with hardly a wrinkle, and lying in his coffin with his eyes closed, he looked like Buddha. I wept at my father's funeral, though I did not fully understand why.

During most of his time in Guadalupe and during my childhood, my father was a farmer. Anti-Asian alien land laws prohibited him from buying land, but he was able to lease it. He was no dirt farmer. He took pride in never having done any physical labor since he was twenty years old. He drove around inspecting his farms in a big Buick while a foreman or one of his sons supervised the Mexican work gangs. There were times he would go to work in a three-piece suit with a gold watch chain looping from his vest pocket, and in the evening, he would come tramping home with mud on his brown, pointy shoes. The butt of a White Owl cigar would be in his mouth and a light brown fedora on his head.

My mother would be extremely agitated when Papa was in a bad mood, but sometimes I would miss the warning signs and let slip an incautious word or gesture that would touch off my father's explosive temper. Those times were actually rare, but they stick in my mind. My father told me about a samurai who asked his young son which parent he liked better, him or his mother. The boy, with some subtle prodding from his mother, said he loved his father better, whereupon the samurai drew his sword and decapitated the boy. "I will not have a liar for a son," he said. When my father asked me whom I liked better, him or my mother, I said I liked them both the same. That was also a lie, but it satisfied my father.

My brothers and sisters used to say that Papa was not nearly as strict with me as he had been with them and that he spoiled me because I was the baby of the family. When I was very young, perhaps three or four, he would take me into his bed and hug me like a rag doll. I got no pleasure from that. Papa's breath smelled of cigars, and his cheeks, pressed against mine, felt like a wire brush. He often laughed about how I, when still an infant, urinated in his face while he was changing my diapers. As I got older, he stopped being physically affectionate but instead brought home toys—motorboats, tricycles, cap pistols, toy swords. I did not like receiving these gifts from him; my feelings towards him were dominated more by fear than love.

I can still see my father sitting at the table after dinner, pushing back his chair, unbuttoning his vest, and lighting up a cigar. He held his cigar with his left hand and patted his belly with his right as he talked. He looked fatter than he actually was because in summer and winter he wore a belly wrap, a long, heavy piece of flannel that he would wind several times around his body. He said the secret to good health was to keep your belly warm. His huge head, which he kept closely cropped, added to the feeling I always had when I was with him of a very large presence. His jowls gave his head the shape of an eggplant, and his big ears shot up from them like pink butterflies. I saw my father as godlike: unpredictable and unknowable. Once, in a Kabuki performance, he played the role of a samurai disguised as a peasant. In the climactic scene, the peasant robes fell away and he was revealed as a warrior. Standing on stage with his ferociously painted face, in magnificent red and gold armor and swinging a huge shining sword, he was at once beautiful and terrifying. That, it seemed to me, was the essence of my father who walked about in the white man's world dressed in a business suit and smoking a cigar. If I liked my father at all, it was from a safe distance, when his mind was wandering elsewhere, away from me. He was a passionate reader of Japanese history, and in an expansive mood, he would tell stories about famous samurai heroes. In an especially good mood, he would tell stories about his youth and about his early days in America. The stories were told in bits and pieces and he repeated them in no particular order. When we had sukiyaki for dinner, he told of how he went with friends to a restaurant in Kumamoto City when he was a student. "We ordered sukiyaki because it was made of beef, and we wanted to know what it was like. They came with a big platter filled with white meat. It became transparent as it was cooked. 'Ho,' we said, 'so this is what beef is like.' It was delicious. It was the most delicious meal I had ever had. It was only after I came to America that I realized that what they had given us was pure fat, just hunks of suet sliced up like meat. They knew students wouldn't know the difference." When we had fish for dinner, he would tell how he and his brothers, when they were children, used to quarrel over who had the biggest piece. I did not fully understand that story, because unlike the people of Japan, we always had plenty to eat, and I was not overly fond of fish.

My father came from the southern island of Kyushu. His father was a wholesale fish merchant in the small village of Nagasu on Ariake Bay. When he was a boy, whales would come into the bay. "We ran down the street telling everyone that 'kujira-san' was here. We said kujira-san, not just kujira, because we didn't want to offend such big fish, but then the kujira stopped coming into the bay. People said it was because of the new steamships that went by the mouth of the bay on their way to Kagoshima. But it wasn't the steamships; the kujira stopped coming because there weren't many fish left to feed on in the bay." As fishing in the bay declined, so did my grandfather's business. In an attempt to save it, he invested in a big net, and when that enterprise failed, he was deeply in debt. My father, the second son, went to America in the hope of paying off his father's debts. That he managed to do this was his proudest accomplishment. He often mentioned how he enabled his father to walk around Nagasu again with his head up.

When my father arrived in San Francisco in 1903, he did not know a soul. He had taken two years of English as a student in Kumamoto City, but his teacher, a Japanese, taught a unique pronunciation used nowhere else in the world. As it turned out, he did not know a word of English anybody could understand. For example, my father never learned, never even tried to learn, to pronounce words beginning with "th" correctly. He had been taught to pronounce such words as if they started with an s. He also had difficulty pronouncing r's and l's, but a more serious problem was his reluctance to end a word with a consonant. How he ever got anybody to understand him was a wonder to me. When I was a child, white men would come over to the house to talk business and I would hear my father say something like, "Nexto monsu (next month), we begin sheening (thinning) lettuce. We have maybe sahty (thirty) acres." Over the years, the white people who did business with people from Japan apparently had to learn to understand their brand of English, but that was not the case when my father first arrived in San Francisco. He often told of how he went to a laundry after his arrival and tried to explain to the proprietor that he wanted his clothes washed. "Wushi," he said. When that got no response, he said, "kuleenu." Then, in desperation, he consulted his Japanese-English dictionary and came up with "lahn-do-ree." He finally ended up washing his clothes himself.

For years, I had accepted that story at face value, never questioning the absurdity of it. It occurs to me now that if someone walked into a laundry with a pile of dirty clothes, the clerk or proprietor should not have any difficulty understanding what the man wanted. The laundry obviously did not want my father's business because he was Asian. Considering that the place was California and the time was 1903—during a period when anti-Asian agitation on the West Coast was strong—that is not just a possibility, it's a certainty. My father rarely talked about racial prejudice, but he did say that during his first years in Guadalupe all the Japanese bachelors cut each other's hair because white barbers refused them service. He didn't seem angry or bitter about it; he laughed when he talked about it, as if the barber's animosity was what one would expect from a hakujin, a white man. He laughed when he talked about his first job in America. He worked as a dishwasher in a restaurant. It was a good job to begin with, he said, because he was allowed to sleep on the kitchen floor at night.

On his next job as a cook's helper, he was fired the first day because he broke the yolks of the eggs he was told to crack over the griddle. "The cook scraped up all the eggs and threw them in the garbage can," my father said, and telling the story years later, he still seemed appalled by this terrible waste of food that would have been unthinkable in Japan. I don't know why he stuck to the restaurant trade, but he was next hired as a busboy. One of his first tasks was to fill the sugar bowls, a simple enough job except that in Japan he had never seen granulated salt. Seeing the fine, pure white granules, he concluded it was sugar. The boss said, "Go home."

Despite his record, my father appeared to be working his way up in the restaurant business. His next job was as an apprentice waiter. He did better at this job until he noticed that the other waiters were able to carry four bowls of soup at a time, one in each hand and two others balanced on the right arm. He tried to do the same and it worked just fine until he felt the bowls on his arm getting hotter and hotter. By the time he got to the table, the bowls were scorching and he dumped the soup on a customer's lap. "What I didn't notice was that the other waiters put a towel over their arm before they put the soup bowls on it. It was 'Go home' again. I decided San Francisco was not the place for me. I decided to go to the countryside."

He went into the San Joaquin Valley where he got on a

fruit-picking crew. The pay was 75 cents a day and he had to give 15 cents of that to the contractor who provided rice, pickles, soy sauce, and a shack to sleep in. "I was happy because I was finally with other Japanese. Anyway, we were young and we didn't work very hard. When the boss wasn't around, we threw plums at each other."

He eventually worked his way down to Guadalupe in the Santa Maria Valley, where he heard he could get a job harvesting sugar beets. When he inquired at the sugar company, he discovered that the Japanese workers were not yet organized in crews. Much of the sugar beet work in California had been done by the Chinese who had come to this country earlier. But because of the ban on Chinese immigration that began in 1882, the Chinese population was aging. Many of them, moreover, were demanding higher wages and going on strike. My father had been in America for nearly a year by the time he got to Guadalupe so his English had improved to the point where he could make himself understood most of the time. When the boss at the sugar company discovered he was Japanese and spoke English, he asked him to round up a crew of Japanese workers. "He made me supervisor and gave me a horse to ride around on. After that, I never did a day of physical labor. I was always the boss."

To look older, he grew a mustache. He started smoking cigars. "I wanted to look like a big shot." As soon as he could afford it, he went to a tailor in Santa Maria and had a suit made. He bought a horse named Buster. When he went into town, he would give the reins a flick and Buster would charge around like a wild stallion. Everyone thought he was an excellent horseman. They didn't know that Buster was gentle and was just showing off.

My father learned early that appearance was important, sometimes as important as wealth and position. The Japanese who worked on his crew had little formal education. Because they didn't know about bank accounts, they gave him their money to hold. He kept it for them in his own account, so the people at the bank thought he was rich. He never had any problem getting a loan when he needed one. By the time my father was seven years in this country, he was able to start a farm of his own.

He rarely talked about his life as a bachelor, but undesirable elements from the big cities were among the early immigrants from Japan. By the 1890s there were a number of Japanese brothels in San Francisco and Seattle. When I was a child there were two Japanese restaurants in Guadalupe, which my father and other wealthy farmers frequented. They had flirty women who wore their kimono in a disreputable way that exposed the backs of their necks. I suspect they had predecessors who came to Guadalupe in the early days. One of them, it seemed, married and attained some outward respectability. After the war, when I was old enough to understand such matters, my father told me that a certain Mrs. X's five children were each fathered by different men. If there were Japanese women in Guadalupe in the early days, they were not the type that a rising young farmer like my father would marry. So, he wrote to his father in Nagasu to ask him to find him a wife. His father was quick to respond. Within a few months, a young bride arrived at San Francisco.

3

My mother was born in 1893, the third and youngest child of an impoverished samurai living in Kumamoto City, the capital of the prefecture in which my father's village was located. The Meiji Restoration of the 19th century ended the feudal system of Japan and transformed the fiefdoms into civically governed provinces. In the process, the samurai who had been retainers of the deposed provincial lords initially got government stipends, but these were gradually reduced until they were eliminated completely. The high-ranking and well-connected became the elite, political leaders, part of the professional class and civil servants, but many others were impoverished.

Because my mother's father was too poor to keep her, she was adopted by Mr. Ueno, the village photographer in Nagasu. When I was a child, my mother would talk about her childhood from time to time, but unlike my father's stories, hers tended to be unhappy and bitter. She said her hands would get so cold in school that she could hardly hold her pencil. But nobody complained. It was winter and in winter it was supposed to be cold. She never went to school beyond the fifth grade, and although it was rare in those days for a girl to continue school beyond the elementary level, she was angry about it. Perhaps because she was born in a samurai family, my mother had a high opinion of herself despite her childhood poverty. She talked about how in Kumamoto City she had won an essay contest and her essay was read by the teacher to the entire school. Her teacher appeared to have been a progressive thinker, for he told her that in modern Japan, everyone, even girls, could aspire to anything they wanted. "I wanted to be an architect," she used to say with sadness in her voice.

In the family in which she was adopted, my mother said she was treated like a maid. She never told me, if she knew, what the financial arrangements were for her adoption, but her father had been an impoverished samurai who couldn't afford to keep her, so her former social status meant little in her new family. One of her chores was looking after the youngest daughter, a coddled and spoiled child whose hair she had to comb every morning. "A hateful child," my mother said. "She would complain I was hurting her and say she was going to tell her mother on me. She'd make me so mad that I would give the comb another yank and she would cry and run to her mother. A hateful child." The only happy memory she seemed to have of Nagasu was the Kabuki troupe that came once a year to perform. The family would pack a lunch and spend the whole day on the grounds of the Shinto shrine where the plays were performed.

When, as an adult, I asked my mother about her early childhood, she told me she had no memory of her father because he died when she was still a little girl. She remembered her mother, but all she would say about her was, "Oh, she was nice. I liked her." She did tell me, however, about how she came to America. She said my father's father spotted her in a village shop. After making inquiries about her, he sent, as it was the custom at the time, a go-between to visit the girl's family with an offer of marriage. The prospective groom would pay for necessary clothing and all travel expenses, including a first-class ticket. "I accepted," she said, "because I didn't want to be stuck in a little country village like Nagasu. I thought I would like to go to Tokyo one day, but going to America seemed almost as good."

She was a child of seventeen when she sailed for America to marry a man she had never seen. My father met her at the docks in San Francisco. Her first thoughts when she met her prospective husband were, "My, how dark he is." Then she remembered he was a farmer. He must be in the sun a lot. She spent her first night in San Francisco, along with other Japanese brides traveling first class, at a Christian home for girls. My father brought her a box of sushi for dinner, which she recalled with fondness. It is difficult to see your own mother as a dreamy young girl, but perhaps in coming to America she had fantasized a prince who was going to sweep her off her feet and carry her to his castle. She had no doubt heard the stories of the wondrous riches to be had in America and had seen a picture of her prospective groom, who was indeed dressed like foreign nobility. My father's dark complexion must have jolted her back to reality. When I was a child, my mother was apologetic about my dark complexion. "I drank too much tea when I was pregnant with you," she would say. She was also sorry about my low nose and when lying in bed with me she would softly pinch the bridge of my nose and say, "Takonare, takonare" or "May it get higher, may it get higher." A light complexion and a high nose are associated with nobility in Japan. My mother was very fair, but she was ashamed of her low, turned-up nose. My father, on the other hand, had a narrow aristocratic nose, marred only by a slight bump in the middle, but, as my mother observed, had the complexion of a peasant. These attributes were randomly scattered within our family. The oldest daughter, Yoshiko, was a beauty, with a well-shaped oval face, a small but sharp nose and light complexion. Of the boys, Yoshiro was the best looking with a light complexion and a prominent well-formed nose. Everyone said he looked like a samurai. My brother Goro and my sister Hoshiko were also light skinned but had noses much like mine, broad and flat. I had the worst possible combination: a low nose and a dark complexion, a face a mother could love despite its shortcomings.

As a child, still too young to go to school, I followed my mother everywhere and stood beside her while she did her housework. She was always talking to herself, to me, or to the world at large. After I started going to school, I had friends I played with, but I was often sick and she would lie in bed with me and talk in her self-absorbed way. Frequently, she complained about Papa. "He has no business sense," she would say. "Too impatient, too inconstant. If I ran the business, we'd be rich by now." I was like a doll to which a young girl might complain and pour out her troubles. I don't think my mother expected me to understand her muttering, but there was much I did take in because her central complaints were repeated over and over. "Why can't he ever finish what he starts? He'll start a hobby and lose interest. Look at the canary house, the fishpond. The canary house is full of spider webs and the fishpond is stagnant, choked with moss." She even criticized the one enduring hobby my father had, joruri, narrative poetry sung in the classical puppet theater of Japan. My father would practice joruri for hours, alternately pitching his voice high and weeping as a woman and switching to the hero's role and roaring like a bull. My mother listening in the kitchen would shake her head and say, "He practices and practices and never gets any better." My father was greatly handicapped by being tone-deaf.

When my parents married, my father still lived in a bachelor labor camp and that was where he took his bride. They lived in a small three-room house set off from the bachelor quarters. The barracks in these labor camps were usually nothing more than shacks, at times with dirt floors. But the house my father and mother first lived in appeared to have been especially well appointed with a real floor, a wood stove and even running water. My mother recalled with some pride how she learned to hitch a horse to wagon and how she drove alone into town for supplies. The only other woman in the camp was an older person who lived with the camp cook. "I don't think they were married," she told me. "They just lived together. I don't remember her name anymore, but that woman taught me everything, even how to cook rice."

Eventually my father bought a small store in town that the bank put up for sale to satisfy a mortgage forfeiture. He got around the alien land law by buying the property in his son's name. He bought the property to move his growing family into town where they could have hot and cold running water and piped-in gas and electricity, but he soon had a busy general store. My mother started it almost by accident. She said when they first moved in, there was still some merchandise left in the store —canned foods, tobacco and a few items of dry goods—and people would come into the store to buy things. A Mexican would come in, take a bag of tobacco and press a coin in her palm. Even Japanese began popping in to buy a can of this or that. Wholesale salesmen would also drop by, so she started restocking the shelves. Gradually she had a thriving store. Business continued to improve and got so good that my father gave up his farming. He expanded the inventory and even had a gasoline pump installed out front. "I had the first gasoline station in Guadalupe, "he used to say.

My mother looked back to this period of their life with great joy. Half of her customers were Mexicans and they went out of their way to teach her Spanish. "Buenos días, Mama," they would say when they came in. When she raised five fingers, they would say, "Cinco, Mama. Cinco centavos." When she repeated it, they would say, "Bueno! Mama. Muy bueno!" She had no difficulty with the language. It came far easier to her than English ever did or would. She enjoyed herself immensely running the store. "We sold, we sold," she used to say, happy in the memory. "It was fun, we sold so much.'"

Then, one day, fire destroyed the store. The store and invento-ry were insured so the loss was not catastrophic. My mother wanted to rebuild at the same location. "We were right in the center of town," she said. "It was convenient for everybody; that's why business was so good." But my father had bigger ideas. He bought a piece of property on the edge of town where he could build a larger, more elaborate store. "It was too big," my mother said. "The little store we had was just right. People felt comfortable there. The new store was too big for Guadalupe."

Actually, the store was only about 25 feet wide, 50 feet deep and only a half a city block from the center of town. But it was located just beyond where the concrete sidewalk left off and there was only a wooden boardwalk. My mother was no doubt right. The little, hole-in-the-wall, Mama-Papa store smack in the middle of town was just perfect for Guadalupe. But it was 1931, well into the Depression. A fancy new store on the edge of town could not survive. Shortly after I was born, my father closed the business and went back to farming. I don't know if my mother ever forgave him. Her anger was still hot when I was a little boy clinging to her skirt and she railed incessantly about my father's lack of business sense. During my father's later years, I got the impression that he held my mother in awe and always had in spite of the tyrannical way in which he ruled over her. Part of the reason might have been her samurai background. His intense interest in Japanese history and its heroes made such things important to him. But the main reason, I suspect, was that he knew in his heart that she was more intelligent and capable than he. He was in many ways like a petulant child, dependent and demanding. My mother used to say, "I hope he dies before me, because he couldn't take care of himself. Always calling, 'Mama, Mama,' he's as helpless as a child."

Over the years, my father's fortune waxed and waned. He once farmed 1,000 acres and owned a herd of 200 horses. When I was a child, my father was operating on a smaller scale, but he still ran substantial farms at three different locations and had invested heavily in tractors, plows and other modern equipment.

He traded in his Buick every three years for a new one, so with his big, shiny car and his three-piece suits, he looked every bit the "big shot" that he was in the Japanese community. In our living room were trophies and gold cups given to my father for his services as chairman or vice chairman of the Farmers' Association, the Japanese School Committee and various other community organizations and fundraising drives. The most important people in Guadalupe, all farmers, were frequent visitors at our house.

We ate well in our family. For breakfast there was fried rice, eggs, bacon, sausage, buttered toast and on Sundays heaps of pancakes. We bought rice in hundred-pound sacks, soy sauce by the barrel and my mother made huge quantities of pickles in the empty barrels. We ate a great deal of fish and were told that in Japan not even the wealthy ate fish so frequently. We ate things that even the rich did not eat—chicken roasted two at a time, steaks, hamburgers, pork chops, roast beef and pork, rich stews with chunks of short ribs. There was usually fruit in the house and milk, which I hated and was required to drink a glass a day. My sister Hiroko was fond of baking so we regularly had cakes and cookies in the house.

I often asked my mother if we were rich and she always gave an ambiguous answer, such as, "We are very fortunate," so that I was never sure. I understand today that there was no easy answer to the question. My father had his good years when he was indeed a wealthy man, but there were also years when he was on the verge of bankruptcy. He was always taking risks, hoping to make a quick fortune. The farmers who did best in Guadalupe grew lettuce year after year because there was a steady market for it. But my father gambled with less reliable crops, always hoping to hit it big. He once even bought stock in a silver mine in Nevada, an investment he did not like to be reminded of.

In 1940, after nearly four decades in America, my father was still trying to make his fortune. He thought of himself as a transient even though his children were being educated in American schools and he had two sons in Stanford University. At home we had all the modern conveniences: a washing machine, a Hoover vacuum cleaner, a gas range and an electric ice box. We had a piano, a phonograph, a radio console and ornate Victorian furniture, but all in a chicken-coop house that swayed in the wind and was gnawed through by rats. It was the Japanese version of the American dream. Like most Japanese immigrants, my father was not at home in the United States and the country did everything it could to keep him feeling that way. Anti-Japanese agitation led to a total ban on immigration from Japan in 1924. Japanese nationals already in the country were denied naturalization privileges and many western states passed laws that prohibited "aliens ineligible for citizenship" from owning land and that limited the length of leases. Japanese businessmen and farmers, like my father, found ways of getting around these restrictions, but these and other attempts at oppression kept alive their yearning to return one day to their homeland. Many did return. My father stayed on because even as an unwelcome guest he had a better life and more opportunities in America than he could have dreamed of in Japan. Torn between gratitude and resentment, he was bound to America by his aspirations and by his children, who year by year became increasingly unfit for life in Japan.

4

When my father first came to Guadalupe in 1904, the only Japanese who were there were young men looking for work. Over the years, the Japanese community grew steadily. By the 1930s, when I was growing up, Japanese accounted for nearly a quarter of the approximately 2,400 people living in and around Guadalupe. Although we were a minority, it seemed to me as a child that Guadalupe was a Japanese town, so self-contained and self-sufficient was our community.

We lived, however, in a way that was neither entirely Japanese nor American. Our life was a random mixture of East and West. Some days, the food would be purely Japanese, but on others we might have spaghetti and rice, or corned beef and cabbage and rice. It would not have been unusual for one of us to put catsup on the rice and soy sauce on the spaghetti. After school I might have a rice ball wrapped in seaweed for a snack, or it might be a peanut butter and jelly sandwich, or a fried tortilla buttered and sprinkled with sugar. When we played, I might strap on a six-shooter and be a cowboy or stick a wooden samurai sword in my belt. At Christmas we put up a Christmas tree and before New Year's Day we pounded hot rice into a sticky glutinous mass called mochi, a traditional Japanese New Year's food. Two large mochi patties with a tangerine on top would be placed on the piano as an offering to Shinto gods. At Easter we colored eggs and on Thanksgiving Day we had turkey. On Buddha's birthday we celebrated the flower festival and during the Bon festival, wearing kimono, we danced around a bonfire to the beat of a taiko drum and the blaring of odori music. Japanese Boy Scouts would march in the Fourth of July parade and on the Emperor's birthday gather at the Seinen-en-Dan, the young men's association hall, and shout "banzai!" to wish the Emperor long life.

The Seinen Dan was used as a judo and kendo (fencing) training hall and also doubled as a movie theater where Japanese films were shown. The children also went to the Royal Theater for American movies, usually to the Saturday matinee. My parents took us occasionally to the theaters in nearby Santa Maria when a major film such as *Gone With The Wind* or *Romeo and Juliet* came. I don't think they understood such films very well, but they seemed to think we ought to participate in the local cultural life in much the same way that they, when they were children in Japan, were taken to see the traveling Kabuki troupe perform. What my father really liked were Charlie Chaplin films. My mother favored Shirley Temple.

At home we got *The Los Angeles Times* and *Life* magazine, Japanese ethnic newspapers from Los Angeles and San Francisco and an array of magazines from Japan, some of which dealt with politics and world affairs while others provided household and fashion tips, children's games and stories. We had many of the popular Japanese records at home and heard others played at the Seinen-Dan on movie nights. We also listened to the Hit Parade on the radio, so as a child I knew the words of most American as well as Japanese hits. This meshing of cultures came about naturally enough, but the American element came mainly from my older siblings. My brother Yoshiro was a Boy Scout and one of his most treasured memories was of the time he went to a Boy Scout jamboree in Washington, D.C., where he was among a group of Scouts who met President Roosevelt. He had a childhood dream of going to Stanford University and playing on the varsity football team. He kept a scrapbook of newspaper clippings of the Stanford football team and did stretching exercises to grow taller. He did manage to go to Stanford but remained too small to try out for football. My sister Hoshiko was required to take Japanese dance lessons, which she hated. As a compromise she was allowed to take tap dancing lessons as well. She was also a member of the high school majorette team and for a time practiced twirling the baton every day. When her fingers blistered, she would wrap them with Band-Aids. For Hoshiko, performing a Japanese dance on stage at the Seinen-Dan dressed in kimono was agony, but marching down Main Street in the Fourth of July parade wearing a short, flounced skirt and white cowboy boots was a joy.

Hoshiko, being seven years older than I, distinguished more sharply between Japanese and American ways. She hated it when Papa and Mama talked about going back to Japan someday and nothing upset her more than having to behave like a demure Japanese girl. She was always practicing her tap-dancing steps in the living room, singing, "I'm nobody's baby now…" Her proudest moment was when, after she started attending high school, she got her first permanent wave, something no respectable girl her age would have been allowed to do in Japan. As an adult, I understood that Hoshiko, being seven years older than I, knew her Japanese cultural training was to prepare her to someday be a Japanese bride. When my parents spoke of returning to Japan, she would whisper under her breath, "I don't want to go to Japan! I don't want to…"

I, on the other hand, felt at home in both cultural settings. I had samurai and cowboy heroes. My first language was Japanese, but after I began school and became fluent in English I could easily slide from one language to the other. I was, however, made aware very early of the tension between America and Japan. When I was perhaps six years old, my mother laid down a Japanese magazine she was reading and murmured, "I hope it never happens." "What, Mama?" I asked. "What never happens?" My mother muttered to herself the way she often did. It was a difficult Japanese phrase. "What, Mama?" I persisted. "What never happens?" Finally, she said, "War. War between Japan and America. But don't worry, Gene, it won't happen." Despite this reassurance I was stunned. As a child, I lived happily in the merged world of Japan and America. That was the universe in which I existed. That the two should clash was unthinkable. It felt like being thrown into utter darkness. I struggled to get the thought out my mind while my mother kept assuring me that it would never happen.

When I look back on it today, there were distinct signs of impending war between Japan and America beginning in the late 1930s and early 1940s. There were Japanese troops in China, which I was aware of even as a child. There were daily reminders of them-in the newsreels, the songs we sang and heard, in the magazines we got from Japan. The children's magazines often had cartoons of Chinese children waving Japanese flags and welcoming the invading army. The Chinese leaders were said to be so corrupt that the Chinese people welcomed the Japanese soldiers as friends and liberators. My mother used to coax me into eating misoshiru, a murky brown soup made with fermented soybean paste, saying it was what made Japanese soldiers strong. My father had a large map of world, which he put up on the living room wall. The map showed Japan and all its conquered territories in red. "Look at what a tiny country Japan is," he would say, "and look at all the territories she has." When President Roosevelt spoke on radio, we all sat in the living room and listened. My father's English was not up to understanding a presidential speech, so one of my brothers would have to translate. "There, he said something about Japan," my father would say. "What is he saying about Japan?"

Later, a special envoy came from Japan for peace talks in Washington. We saw pictures of him and the Japanese ambassador in American newspapers. We also saw them in Japanese and American newsreels. It was clear that things were not well between the United States and Japan.

Listening to the Army-Navy game on the radio one day, I heard the midshipmen shouting, "Sink the Army! Sink the Army!" Being an Army rooter, I began shouting, "Sink the Navy! Sink the Navy!" My sister Hiroko swooped down on me. "Don't say that, Gene," she said. "What would people think if they heard you?" I was indignant. If Navy rooters could shout, "Sink the Army, I certainly ought to be able to retaliate in kind. Recently, I called the Naval Academy in Annapolis and inquired when the Army-Navy game was played in 1941. It was played on Saturday, November 29, eight days before the Japanese attack on Pearl Harbor.

On December 7, 1941, my father came home in the evening looking flushed and told Mama that he and some of the others met at the Japanese Farmers' Association office and shouted "banzai" to the Emperor. He laughed, but there was no humor in his laughter. My mother did not laugh, nor did she respond. She seemed very distant. That night, in the early morning hours of December 8, two FBI agents came to our house and arrested my father. He was one of several hundred previously identified Japanese leaders living on the West Coast who were arrested within 24 hours of the outbreak of the war. The FBI was obviously well prepared and ready to act within hours if a war broke out. My father, like the others, was never charged with any crime. He was arrested and interned because he was a leader in the Japanese community. We were not to see him for two years.

I had slept through my father's arrest. Hoshiko told me about it in the morning. She pointed to the telephone on the kitchen wall. The FBI men had cut the cord of the receiver before they left so we would not be able to tell anybody that they were coming. The FBI cutting the telephone cord had more of an immediate emotional impact on me than their arresting my father. It was tangible evidence that the American government saw us as enemies. For days, I kept glancing at the severed cord hanging lifelessly against the kitchen wall. Eventually somebody came and fixed it.

A few weeks later, we got a letter from my father. It was sent from the Santa Barbara County Jail, where, he told us later, he and the others were fed on bread and water and interrogated for several days. They thought they were going to be executed. My father did not say so in his letter, but he did not expect to see us again.

My mother went around with her brow furrowed. She seemed detached and remote. Her hair began to turn gray. For years, I imagined that my mother's hair had turned white overnight. But now I recall that my mother used to dye her hair. A more plausible explanation is that she simply stopped dying her hair. But she was being crushed by fear and worry for her husband and her children. I heard her crying at night. She thought the FBI agents would come again at any moment. Like most farmers, we had guns in the house, .22s and shotguns. My mother told Nimashi to bury them in a ravine behind one of our farms. My father's samurai sword, a relatively worthless curio he had picked up in Los Angeles, was also broken in two and buried. Cameras were suspect, so we threw them away. There were no more visits by the FBI or police and I don't recall any anti-Japanese incidents occurring in Guadalupe, but my mother no longer felt safe in town, so we moved to one of our farms where Hiroko and her husband lived with their baby daughter.

They lived four miles out of town. The house was far off the road and partly obscured by a ring of eucalyptus and fruit trees. Gray-brown stretches of plowed fields surrounded the house so that it looked like a fortress set in an oasis. There was plenty of room in the spacious, two-story house. It was solidly built, with a big kitchen, a formal dining room, a living room with a fireplace and six bedrooms. It was the best house my mother ever lived in or ever would, but she seemed scarcely aware of her surroundings. Most of time, she just sat in an armchair in the living room staring at the floor. It was a lonely time for me because I had to catch the bus after school and could not stay to play with my friends. My father's Mexican foreman lived with his son in a small shack-like house on the other side of the barn. I played with the boy now and then, but he was several years older than I and a bully so I did not like him much. My best friend was Jackie, my brother-in-law's German shepherd. He was kept chained to an apricot tree near the entrance of the house. The dog weighed almost as much as I did and we spent a lot of time wrestling.

I was elated when we moved back into town in the summer of 1942, but our homecoming turned out to be only temporary. I soon found out that the reason we returned to Guadalupe was to prepare for "the evacuation." My mother bought me a pair of cowboy boots, which, of course, made me very happy. It was said that we were being sent to a desert, so many Japanese children were now wearing cowboy boots-to protect against snake bites. Adults were buying knee-high "engineer's boots" and pith helmets.

After the attack on Pearl Harbor there were many stories about the cruel and treacherous nature of Japanese in the newspapers and magazines. They depicted Japanese as subhuman creatures, most often as apes and they made no distinction between the Japanese of Japan and those of us in the United States. A phrase that was often heard was, "A jap is a jap." Another phrase that was quoted in the newspapers was, "A good jap is a dead jap." I had difficulty understanding the latter phrase because like most children I tended to be literal minded and a stranger to irony. How could a dead person be a good person?

Racist attitudes were common and universally accepted in those days; they were simply part of the communal way of looking at the world. People of different races were not intended to mix. The Japanese living in America were no different. My mother used to say she had difficulty dealing with hakujin (literally, white people) because they all looked alike. The hakujin portrayed in the Japanese children's magazines had pasty, white complexions, almost like painted Kabuki actors and enormous beak-like noses. In their ghostly appearance, they all did look alike. When Japanese said "hakujin" there was usually a twist to it. Sometimes there was contempt in the word, sometimes admiration, sometimes mystification. One element that was always there, was the unspoken understanding that hakujin were different from us, as were, of course, the Mexicans, the Filipinos and the Chinese who lived in Guadalupe.

The one place where this separation of the races tended to break down was the school. Most of the children were white, but Japanese were the largest minority and there were a number of Mexican children. Most of the teachers had taught there for years. My mother didn't refer to teachers as hakujin; she called them sensei, which means teacher but is also a term of affection and respect. She knew some of them by name. She used to say what a sweet, clever child Mrs. Negrich, the kindergarten teacher, used to be. We apparently had had business dealings with her family at one time. Mr. Johnson, the principal, was a symbol of power and authority in our house. My brothers and sisters continued to speak of him with awe even after they left the school. Mr. Johnson had the reputation of being especially mean and tough. My brother Yoshiro often talked about how he once saw Mr. Johnson grab two Mexican boys by their collars and throw them down the stairs. He was not as rough with white and Japanese children but they also got their share of head slaps and paddling. One of the ways a new child was initiated to the school was to be taken past Mr. Johnson's office. Through the open door, you could see a wooden paddle hanging on the wall by a leather strap.

Although white, Japanese and Mexican children tended to remain apart outside of school, we played together during recess and lunchtimes. There was a Portuguese boy with whom I played a lot at school and I even visited him a few times at his home.

The Guadalupe Joint Union Grammar School, as it was officially called, was the one place the war did not change. After the attack on Pearl Harbor, Mr. Johnson called an assembly to tell the faculty and the children that the Japanese children were Americans like everybody else. He didn't want the word, "jap," used in the school. It's not that much trouble to say Japanese, he said. Although radio, the movies and the newspapers bombarded the public daily with the word, "jap," I never heard it used in the Guadalupe grammar school during the months following the outbreak of the war.

We began to sell "liberty stamps" at school to help finance the war. Mrs. McDermott, our third-grade teacher, made me and another Japanese boy co-chairmen of the drive. Every week, we would take the money we collected in class to the post office to buy the stamps. There were two posters at the post office. One had a picture of Hitler with the words, "Today Germany. Tomorrow the world." The other had three rats with the faces of Hitler, Mussolini and Tojo. I bought stamps, too, with the money my mother gave me. She said saving money was always good no matter how you did it. She chuckled as she said it, but the irony passed over my head at the time.

After the Japanese were ordered out of the West Coast and we were preparing to be shipped to somewhere in the wilderness, Mrs. Abernathy and Miss Kennedy came to our house. We had a picture of them, taken at some outing, in our family album so we apparently knew them better than the other teachers. Mrs. Abernathy, who taught the sixth grade, was a huge, tank-like woman who maintained order with a yardstick. My brother Yoshiro often talked about the time Mrs. Abernathy told him to hold out his hand for some misbehavior. At the last moment, he could not stop himself from withdrawing his hand, causing the yardstick to swish harmlessly by. "Boy, did she let me have it the second time," he recalled. Miss Kennedy had been my second-grade teacher and she, too, was a strict disciplinarian. She kept a leather strap nailed to a wooden handle in her desk drawer. When there was a fight or unruly behavior in the playground, it was enough for Miss Kennedy to walk out with her leather strap in hand to restore order. I was alarmed to see these two formidable women come into our house. My sister Hiroko and her family had moved to our house in Guadalupe to prepare for the evacuation, so she was there to talk to the two teachers. The teachers remembered Hiroko from her school days and told her with tears in their eyes that what the government was doing was wrong. They said they were sorry and they wished there was something they could do. Then, with nothing more to be said, they each embraced Hiroko and left. I witnessed it all from a safe distance and was relieved to see them go.

5

The house was crowded the night before we left Guadalupe because the Tomookas, a family with seven children who lived on a farm miles out of town, came to spend the night. The Tomooka parents were also natives of Nagasu and Mrs. Tomooka was my father's cousin, so we were close to them. Because there were not enough beds for everyone, the younger children slept on the floor and we thought that was great fun. Tom Tomooka was my age and in the morning he and I helped stack the mattresses. Afterwards we climbed on top and jumped and tumbled on them until Mrs. Tomooka came and told us to stop. That is the last clear memory I have of "the evacuation." When I try to recall the day we left Guadalupe it is like trying to bring back a dream. I retain a few vague images and I sense there are others lurking close to the surface, but just beyond my grasp. All the families were assigned numbers which they wrote on baggage tags. I remember my mother putting a numbered tag on me.

To this day, I do not remember how we were transported out of Guadalupe. It was decades after the event that I came across a video documentary, a collection of home movies made of life in the camps by inmates who against orders had managed to smuggle in a camera. The work, *Something Strong Within,* written by Robert A. Nakamura, opened with amateur film made in March of 1942 in Guadalupe of armed soldiers loading Japanese and their baggage onto Greyhound buses. It was credited to Franklin Johnson, Superintendent of the Guadalupe School District, but he was no doubt our Mr. Johnson, the fearsome principal we all remember.

I thought it strange that I could not remember how we were transported out of Guadalupe. But even my mother and my sisters, when I asked them years later, said they could not remember. It was only then that I began to realize how traumatized we must have been to have suppressed so completely the memory of what had to have been the most deeply frightening moment in our lives.

The camp at Tulare, built on the county fairgrounds, was colorless and barren with row after row of tar-papered barracks. Officially designated as an "assembly center," it was surrounded by two high barbed-wire fences. Soldiers carrying rifles with fixed bayonets patrolled the area between the two fences. Some of us children tried at first to make friends with them. We walked up to the fence and said, "Hi," but we got no response. The soldiers were sullen, even hostile, so we gave up on that effort. There were guard towers along the perimeter of the camp each with a searchlight and a 50-caliber machine gun, the kind with barrels that look like large rolling pins. The searchlights were used after dark to sweep the fences should there be an attempt to escape.

According to the date on Mr. Johnson's film, it was still spring, but I recall the atmosphere as dusty, hot and oppressive. A dull, oily smell from the tar paper hung in the air everywhere, both indoors and out. A fine dust covered the ground. As you walked there would be white puffs rising around your feet. It seeped into the barracks through the cracks in the floor and covered everything with a powdery film.

My mother, my sixteen-year-old sister Hoshiko, my oldest brother Nimashi—then a young man of twenty-nine— and I shared a twelve-by-twenty-foot compartment. The barracks had no ceilings and the walls between compartments did not go all the way to the roof, so you could hear everything that was said in the adjoining compartments. The couple next door frequently fought. The wife would say, "Everybody can hear you." And the husband would say, "I don't give a damn. Let them hear." When he wanted quiet, though, he expected us to be considerate of him. When I got an ear infection and lay moaning on my cot, he said, "Can't you shut that kid up? How can anybody sleep with that noise?" My mother said, "I'm terribly sorry, but the child has an earache. Please forgive us," but he continued to grumble.

After a few weeks, my two other brothers, Yoshiro and Goro, who had been students at Stanford, joined us and there was barely room enough to hold the cots. When they arrived in Tulare, Hoshiko stood apart and cried. If we had been a white family, we would have hugged and kissed each other, but Japanese, even the second-generation, nisei, were restrained, except for me. I jumped up and down. The others just smiled while Hoshiko stood apart and wept.

The women suffered most from the lack of privacy. The communal showers and toilets were without partitions and the women, particularly nisei less accustomed to hardships than their mothers, experienced them as a form of debasement. Many waited until late at night to go to the latrine or to the shower house, but discovered that others also had the same idea. The toilets were large sewer pipes with four holes cut into them. On one end there was an overhead water tank, which, when released, would send the water to clear the excrement from below all the holes. One soon learned not to sit at the last hole in the row, for when the dirty water hit the far end it would slosh up through the opening. Most of the time, though, the water pressure was not strong enough, so the latrines were usually filthy, smelled and swarmed with flies. Even today, when under stress, I dream of filthy toilets filled and covered with human feces.

Three times a day there would be loud clanging from the mess hall where a cook beat on a slab of iron to summon us for our meals. We would file in holding forth an empty metal tray on which unsmiling white men ladled small mounds of food. Everything tasted tinny. We had canned wieners and canned vegetables and the juices from them would flow together and form a tepid soup that I mopped up with a piece of bread. As bad as the food was, we were hungry enough to want more. Some of us children would eat quickly and run to another mess hall and get a second meal. Eventually the authorities wised up and issued passes so that we could eat only at our assigned mess hall.

Even as we arrived in Tulare, camps were being built in wilderness areas in the interior of the country. We learned early that the people at Tulare would be going to Arizona, to a place on the Gila River. There were mixed reports as to whether the Gila River had any water in it, but the children talked excitedly about going swimming and fishing. Before we left Tulare, we took our cots and blankets to a storage shed. The women passed a broom around and swept out the compartments. It did not seem to matter to them that the barracks had served their purpose and would be torn down as soon as we left.

The first part of the trip to Arizona was slow because at every depot the train would stop, move on to a siding and sit there for no apparent reason. Some of the military guards would go outside, stand around and smoke cigarettes, but we were required stay in our seats with shades drawn. While the train was stopped at the station, we were not allowed to go to the restroom.

I did not witness it myself, but a story that spread later was about an eccentric old bachelor who tried during one of the stops to go to the toilet. When he was stopped by a military guard, he took a rolled newspaper from under his arm, spread it on the aisles and said in very loud voice so all could hear, "Very well. I will do it here." When he unbuttoned his trousers and squatted, the guard, taken aback and thoroughly flustered, allowed the old man to proceed to the toilet. True or not, the story spread quickly. It was perhaps more embarrassing than inspiring, but it was also a victory, a much-needed morale booster.

Once we got into the desert the train made fewer stops. It was hot, but we were told not to open the windows. A Japanese man with a blue armband came and distributed salt tablets, which we were advised to take. They made me nauseous. A child threw up and I could smell the vomit.

We went to the dining car for meals and the people were pleased that the food was better than at Tulare. But the food that the soldiers got looked better than ours. The Negro waiters, who smiled and joked with the soldiers, were surly when they served the Japanese. They plunked our plates on the table without looking. As if they were feeding animals, somebody said.

In the postwar years a few outspoken Japanese made nuisances of themselves by insisting that we were not "evacuated," which was the official word used, but we were incarcerated, imprisoned. We were not put in "assembly centers" and "relocation centers," we were put in concentration camps. That was not what most Japanese wanted to hear even years after the war. Back in 1942, when we were being "evacuated" and "relocated," we were even less willing to believe that we were being put in concentration camps, despite the bayonets, the barbed wire, the machine guns and searchlights of Tulare and military policemen guarding us on the train. The government made it forcefully clear that we were being imprisoned because of our race, but that was not something most of us wanted to think about.

It was late at night when we got to the Arizona border. "Needles," the people said. Most of the Japanese had never been to Arizona, but everybody seemed to know that Needles was the point of entry. The train stopped for a long time there. People said we were taking on water.

I slept with my head on my mother's lap. Now and then, I would wake up and ask, "Mama, are we there yet?" "Soon," she would say. "We'll be there soon. Go back to sleep." At daylight, the train was still moving through the desert. The land was dotted with sagebrush as far as the eye could see. Here and there were gnarled, leafless trees and giant fork-shaped cactus.

When we first caught sight of Phoenix it looked like an oasis. From the train window, we could see neat, red-tiled houses shaded by palm trees. I hoped that we would live in one of them, but when we got to the Phoenix train station, we were loaded on buses which took us immediately out of town. I kept looking for the river but saw none.

The barracks at Gila had red-shingled roofs and white plasterboard walls, so they looked more cheerful than those in Tulare even though the design and construction were the same. The ground was still carved up by trenches for water and sewer lines and the air was misty with dust. Now and then a whirlwind would form mysteriously and looking like a miniature tornado would zigzag across an open space and break up into clouds of dust as it hit the barracks. Tumbleweed rolled in from the desert and bounced through the camp. There were mounds of baggage on the ground outside one of the barracks that was being used as a bus station. Because of the dust some people wore handkerchiefs and bandannas over their noses like cowboy bandits as they walked around sorting out their possessions.

Our address at Gila was 72-12-A, which meant we were in Block 72, Barrack 12, compartment A. As in Tulare, six of us, my mother, my three brothers, my sister and I, shared one compartment. My sister Hiroko, her husband Nobuo and their baby daughter had a smaller compartment next to ours. We each had a bed frame, a mattress and two drab olive blankets that had "U.S." on them. There was an oil heater in each of the compartments. That was the extent of the furnishings.

It was summer and hot, but cooler at night. The sky was

perfectly clear and at nightfall I looked up and saw more stars than I had ever seen in my life. They were larger and brighter than in California and one stretch of sky looked like somebody had spilled a trail of glistening talcum powder.

My brothers chose to sleep outside in the open air, but I did not join them. I worried about wolves, coyotes, rattlesnakes and scorpions. During the first weeks at Gila, I was insanely afraid of rattlesnakes. I was afraid to go out at night for fear that one would come slithering out from under the barracks. Once, returning from the latrine at night, I fell into a trench and lost my sandals in the loose dirt. While looking for my sandals I was overcome by panic, for I was sure a rattler lurked there somewhere. I leaped out of the trench and ran barefoot as fast as I could to our quarters.

At Gila there were no barbed wire fences or soldiers with guns. Instead, the desert and all its deadly creatures held us prisoner. It took several weeks before I could go into the desert without peeking under bushes, ready to run at the first sign of movement.

Those first few weeks in Gila made a lasting impression. Even fifteen years later, in 1958, imaginary desert creatures haunted me. At the time, I was going to the University of California in Berkeley. I had trouble finding an apartment because many landlords did not want to rent to a Japanese. Eventually, I found a small place in a residential area high in the Berkeley hills. I was depressed at the time because the girl I had hoped to marry had written to me to say she was not coming to Berkeley in the summer as she had said she would. Instead, she was going to New York and perhaps get a job there. I felt betrayed and wrote her a long letter telling her so. It was late at night, but I wanted to mail the letter right away. When I opened the door, however, it seemed to me that there were wild animals roaming around outside, perhaps mountain lions. Fog obscured the streetlight so that it gave off only a dim glow and I could not make out the outlines of the mailbox that I knew was no more than fifty yards away. I closed the door and sat at my desk and smoked a cigarette hoping to get hold of myself. Finally, I decided to mail the letter in the morning and went to bed. I was awakened by a cold draft blowing in my face. It was already light and I could see that the wind had blown the door open. "My God," I thought, "the lions could have come and got me while I slept." The fear had been real. There really seemed to be mountain lions outside, hiding in the azaleas and the rhododendrons in this residential neighborhood. I wondered whether I had gone temporarily insane. It is only in recent years, as I explored my recollections from the camp years, that I have begun to understand that my wartime fears ran deep and that they bubble to the surface from time to time when under stress.

Food was even more scarce at the Gila than at Tulare. Even so, my mother never ate her portion of bread. Instead, she dried it in the sun or toasted it over the oil stove, crumbled it and squirreled it away in brown paper bags. For months, we had bags and bags of dried breadcrumbs stashed in our compartment for when, my mother feared, the food supply would be cut off altogether. It was only in the middle of the second year, when food became more plentiful, that my mother started eating her portion of bread. She finally threw away the bags of breadcrumbs, but she agonized for a long time before she did it.

My mother was not the only one to save breadcrumbs in the early months. It seemed to have been a common practice among the old folks. We children, in contrast, were more concerned with the present hunger. We filched potatoes from the storage shed, packed them in mud and baked them in the desert over an open fire. My brother Yoshiro knew somebody who worked in the kitchen and on two occasions brought back some bread and eggs. We had a small bottle of relish so Yoshiro made omelets on the hot plate. There was enough for each of us to have half a sandwich. I ate mine slowly so that it would last longer. Later, as the food supply increased, the nagging hunger in my belly went away, but the meals I remember are the desert-baked potatoes and the omelet sandwich.

There were people in Congress, such as Representative Martin Dies of Texas, chairman of the House Un-American Activities Committee, who were concerned that the authorities were "coddling" the Japanese in these camps. They worried about "fat-waisted japs" enjoying themselves on American taxpayers' money. The camps were managed by the newly created War Relocation Authority, but Dies wanted them turned over to the Army, which he assumed would be tougher on the japs.

I learned of the views of Mr. Dies and of his colleagues 23 years later while doing research in the library of The Baltimore Sun. I found several brief Sun dispatches out of Washington which quoted Dies and others. The Congressmen seemed to think we were prisoners of war. I was a reporter for The Sun at the time, a free man and not as helpless as I was in 1942, but still those dispatches out of Washington sent a quiver up my back. White people wanted to get back at us for Pearl Harbor and atrocities committed by Japanese troops against American prisoners of war. Vengeance was a motive I could understand, for vendettas were common in the samurai stories my mother used to read to me. The sole purpose in life for Tange Sazen, a one-eyed, one-armed samurai, was to avenge his father's death. One of the most famous stories in Japanese history is that of the 47 ronin, who sacrificed their lives to avenge the death of their lord. And what was the Lone Ranger's main purpose in life if not revenge? In camp, without being conscious of what I was doing, I began distancing myself emotionally from my Japanese identity.

In Tulare one night, there was a talent show at the grandstand where a makeshift stage was built. A matron from Los Angeles sang "Shina-no-yoru," a popular Japanese song at the time. A man from Hawaii regaled the audience with a hula and a boy played a trumpet solo. The big production number of the evening was a chorus line of teenage bobbysoxers. They danced, lip-synching to a recording of the Andrew Sisters—it might have been "Don't Sit Under the Apple Tree." Many in the audience were embarrassed.

The older, parent generation was troubled by this brazen display of American culture. Younger people were also troubled. I heard one young woman say it was difficult for Japanese girls, with their short, daikon (Japanese radish) legs, to carry off a dance hakujin do so well.

After the show, when people began to file out of the grandstand, another boy and I took pebbles off the ground and hurled them into the crowd. I didn't know why I was doing this, but it gave me a terrific feeling of release. Two women walked by and one of them said, "Oh look. Look at the bad boys." But they did nothing to stop us and we kept throwing. When I look back on the incident, it seems to me that it was my way of bombing all Japanese, including those silly bobbysoxers, wearing saddle shoes and doing a hakujin dance with their short, radish-shaped or "daikon" legs. Their desire to express their Americanism was understandable, but to give their hearts and minds to America while in an American prison camp struck me as craven even if I could not have expressed it in that way.

A few months later, at the camp in Gila, Arizona, this confusion over identity continued. There were weekly movies and one night they showed a war film that ended with the sinking of a Japanese battleship. As the American bombs began to explode on the deck of the battleship, the Japanese sailors panicked and leaped into the sea. Young people in the crowd began to giggle and as the ship sank they cheered and applauded. Sitting there in the dark, surrounded by my friends who were shouting, whistling and clapping, I cheered and applauded too. I felt I was doing a bad thing, but it felt good, nevertheless. The parents in the crowd were appalled. Their own children were turning against Japan and if they turned against Japan, they were turning against them. I was aware of that, but I could not stop cheering and applauding.

At Gila, I once saw a teenage boy hurl a rock through a mess hall window. He did not seem to be aiming at anybody, but he had hit a little girl. Two men rushed out of the mess hall and chased the boy across a firebreak. Midway across the field, one of the men managed to kick the boy's feet from under and sent him sprawling. As they led the boy back to the mess hall, one of the men cuffed him on the head. I never found out why the boy did what he did, but I assumed he had no specific reason for throwing the rock; he just wanted to do something bad, just as my friend and I had wanted to do something bad when we threw pebbles into the crowd in Tulare, just as I and perhaps the others had wanted to do something bad when we applauded the sinking of a Japanese battleship. When I think of that today, it strikes me as fear and loathing turned perversely inward and expressed in a confused desire to be liberated and free, not knowing exactly what it was we were trying to escape.

If I had to describe with one word what went on at Gila during the first few months, then that word would be stealing, which went against my strict Confucian upbringing. But morality was turned on its head. My brothers, like everyone else, went to the government storage area at night to steal lumber and any building supplies they could get their hands on. Young men laughed and told stories of how they outwitted the hakujin guys guarding the lumber. There were Japanese guards, too, but they were rarely around when something was being stolen. The stolen lumber became tables, chairs, shelves, closets and dressers. None of my brothers was particularly gifted in woodworking, so our furniture was rough and primitive, but a few compartments eventually had furniture, which, though simple, was as fine as or better than any you could buy.

Partitions materialized in the women's latrines and shower houses. In our block, men built a shaded outdoor sitting area. Young men built gymnastic equipment, horizontal and parallel bars. It was my impression at the time that all the building supplies were stolen, but the authorities probably had to approve some of the projects. An amphitheater was built for movies and Kabuki plays. Baseball diamonds with backstops and basketball courts sprung up on many of the firebreaks.

It was discovered that the castor plant grew quickly and well in that climate, so it was planted by individual families throughout the camp to provide greenery. Some people grew morning glories and trained them on lattices set against the barracks. Later, there were fishponds and rock gardens. Against the summer heat many built coolers, a wooden frame covered with packed straw. Water would be run through the straw and an electric fan placed in the box would draw outside air through the water-soaked straw into the compartment. It had a remarkably cooling effect. From the point of view of basic physical needs, particularly after the first year when the food became minimally adequate, life was not as harsh as one might have expected.

6

During our first year, the burning issue was loyalty, whether we were loyal to Japan or to the United States. Our family, like many others, was split by the issue. My two brothers, Yoshiro and Goro, were pro-American. Simply put, they wanted America to win the war. My oldest brother Nimashi and my brother-in-law Nobuo were kibei—U.S. born Japanese who were educated in Japan. They joined the Seinen-Kai, or young men's association, which was viewed by authorities, and many nisei, as pro-Japan agitators. When Nimashi or Nobuo made what sounded like an anti-American comment, Yoshiro, the most hot-tempered of my brothers, would retort angrily. He would be restrained by Mama from saying more and would go stomping out mumbling under his breath. After a while, Nimashi moved to another block where he lived with friends so we didn't see much of him. Nobuo however, continued to live in the next compartment and the relationship between him and Yoshiro was fraught with unspoken resentment.

One morning on the way to school one of my friends pointed to the top of a nearby butte. There unfurled and waving in the wind was the Hinomaru, a bright red ball on a white field, the flag of Japan. We laughed. We wanted to believe that it was put there as a prank. The thought passed through my mind that Nimashi might have had a hand in it. On the school grounds older students had frowns on their faces in talking in small groups.

When we were sitting in our classroom, Mrs. Smith, our fourth-grade teacher, called me and a girl to her desk. Mrs. Smith was a tall, slender woman probably in her late twenties. She often wore dark glasses, something Japanese rarely did, and was always applying lipstick and powdering her face at her desk. She often looked sad, as if she were trying to overcome a personal sorrow. At times, when the children were busy at their places doing an assignment, she would sit at her desk with her head in her hands, as if asking herself, "What in the world am I doing in a place like this?" She seemed a little cold, as if she didn't like us very much, which made me wonder, too, why she had come to Gila. She might have been married to one of the administrators who lived in a special white people's compound behind the administration building. That would explain how she knew about Nimashi. Mrs. Smith said to the girl, "June, I'm so sorry about your father." June nodded her head and might have said something like, "Oh, that's all right, Mrs. Smith." I thought her father had died. Then Mrs. Smith turned to me and said, "I'm so sorry about your brother." I had not the slightest idea what she was talking about. "Isn't your brother's name Nimashi?" Mrs. Smith asked. I nodded. "You know, don't you?" she said. "He was arrested last night."

Nobuo had been arrested too, and I learned about it only later. Hiroko had another baby shortly after we arrived at Gila and at the time her husband was taken away she was already pregnant with a third. She was normally a cheerful woman who laughed easily, but after Nobuo was arrested her shoulders sagged and she looked tired and worn.

I was aware in a general way of the political controversy raging in the camp. But I didn't talk about it. None of the children did even though we all knew that our older brothers and sisters were arguing about the war and what the government had done to us. While still in Guadalupe, I asked my sister Hoshiko, "You want Japan to win or you want America to win?" I don't remember her answer; she probably didn't give me one. I didn't ask such questions in camp because the loyalty question was splitting our family and I was afraid of it. After Nimashi and Nobuo were taken away I was even more wary of the subject.

During our first year at Gila, the government began allowing people to leave the camps for jobs on the outside if they pledged loyalty to the United States. Yoshiro was the first in our family to leave. He went to Detroit where he worked in a factory. About once a month, he sent us a box full of candy bars, which seemed to me like some fabulous treasure chest. Yoshiro didn't have many friends if any in Detroit and he was lonely. There were race riots there at the time and once a white mob stopped a bus he was riding and dragged a Black passenger out. One of the men in the mob saw my brother and said, "Hey, there's a jap, let's get him." But the others ran off saying, "Naw, we're after niggers tonight." Shortly after that, Yoshiro volunteered for the Army and was sent to Camp Shelby, Mississippi, where an all-nisei combat unit was being trained.

Goro, a pre-med student at Stanford, went to St. Louis where he worked as a laboratory technician at a hospital. The hospital was run by a religious order of brothers and he got along well there, but he was drafted after a few months and like Yoshiro sent to Camp Shelby.

After their arrest, Nimashi and Nobuo were sent to a Department of Justice detention camp in Moab, Utah. Later, Nobuo was allowed to rejoin his family but they were transferred to the Poston, Arizona, camp. None of the so-called "troublemakers" was allowed to return to the camp from which they were removed. Nimashi came to Gila for a brief visit to marry a girl he knew from Guadalupe. After that, he and his bride were sent to the camp at

Manzanar, California.

For me, the loyalty question was like a disease that had infected the family and was eating away at it. It had started with Papa being arrested in the middle of the night. Then, in camp, Nimashi and Nobuo were taken away. Yoshiro and Goro went into the Army. Hiroko and her two children left to join Nobuo at Poston. Hoshiko graduated high school, swore loyalty to the United States and offered a scholarship from Carlton College in Minnesota, she left too. The family was being scattered and perhaps destroyed and the loyalty issue was at the bottom of it.

Many years after the war, when I began reading about our incarceration, I was distressed to see how divisive the loyalty question was to the Japanese community. From the point of view of the government, the issue was settled by summarily putting all of us in concentration camps. Government officials acknowledged some Japanese were probably loyal Americans, but they argued that because of Japanese inscrutability there was no reliable way to weed out the disloyal from the loyal. Most assumed as a matter of faith that there were Japanese, both aliens and American citizens, who, given the opportunity, would commit acts of sabotage and espionage, and when there was no evidence of their doing so, it was taken as an ominous sign. Men such as Earl Warren, then Attorney General of California, and the highly respected columnist Walter Lippmann argued that the absence of overt, hostile acts indicated that the Japanese living in the United States were highly disciplined. They were holding back until a Japanese invasion when they could strike with maximum effect.

Because of the immediate arrest of men such as my father, the Japanese community was left leaderless after the outbreak of the war. The leadership devolved by default on the Japanese American Citizens League, which was made up mainly of college educated, second-generation nisei. Membership was restricted to American citizens. The league leaders initially opposed proposals for "evacuating" everyone of Japanese ancestry from the West Coast. Caught up in the hysteria of the time, one nisei leader, eager to demonstrate Japanese American loyalty, went so far as to propose the creation of a Japanese American "suicide battalion" to fight in the Pacific. After its initial protests, however, the Japanese American Citizens League accepted the conclusion that "the evacuation" of all Japanese, U.S. citizens and aliens alike, from the West Coast was "a military necessity" and cooperated with the program. It even discouraged legal challenges, arguing that cooperating with "the evacuation" was a way for Japanese Americans to demonstrate their loyalty and to contribute to the war effort. After the Japanese were confined behind barbed wire, the league petitioned the government to allow Japanese Americans to volunteer and serve in the armed forces. The league also wanted Americans of Japanese ancestry to be subject to the draft just like everybody else. (After the outbreak of the war, Japanese American were no longer drafted and were not allowed to volunteer for the armed forces.)

Such ultra-patriotism, particularly in a concentration-camp setting, was strongly resented by many, even by those who were fundamentally pro-American. There was also strong suspicion that some league leaders were secretly working with camp authorities and informing on groups and individuals espousing what appeared to be anti-American views. Some of them were set upon and beaten. Ultimately, however, Washington agreed to the creation of a segregated Japanese American combat unit to fight in Europe and reopened the Selective Service System to Japanese Americans.

The War Relocation Authority had previously begun a program for releasing at least a portion of the camp population. Japanese were still banned from the West Coast, but they could be settled in the East. One reason for the program was a habeas corpus case brought by the American Civil Liberties Union representing Mitsuye Endo, one of the inmates, challenging the constitutionality of the imprisonment. Government attorneys seeing the strength of the ACLU's case, wanted to set up a procedure for "sifting" loyal

Japanese Americans from the disloyal so that they would be in a position to demonstrate to the courts that there was a system of due process in place. When the War Department changed its policy on the question of military service for Japanese Americans, the release program was intensified. As a preliminary step, everyone seventeen years and older were required to fill out a questionnaire. Those who formulated the questions were appallingly insensitive to the extraordinary situation in which the Japanese found themselves. U.S. laws did not allow Japanese immigrants, or any Asian immigrants, to become American citizens. In 1922, the Supreme Court had ruled that, naturalization privileges were limited by law to "free white persons and to aliens of African nativity and to persons of African descent." Japanese immigrants could not become American citizens and in spite of that they were asked in the camps to renounce their allegiance to Japan. In effect, to declare themselves stateless persons.

Aside from the loyalty question, most issei did not want to leave the camps for the big cities of the East. Even after decades in America most of them spoke little English and had never lived outside of rural or urban Japanese ghettos on the West Coast. The idea of being cast out to fend for themselves in a strange city full of what were probably hostile white people was understandably frightening to them. As for their children, they were U.S. citizens by birth, but their citizenship, as it turned out, was less important than their race. Now, while imprisoned in camps against their will and in violation of their rights as citizens, they were asked "to serve in the Armed Forces of the United States on combat duty wherever ordered." The authorities, moreover, could not resist asking Japanese Americans to "forswear any form of allegiance or obedience to the Japanese emperor, to any other foreign government, power or organization." This was comparable to asking Joe DiMaggio, the son of Italian immigrants, to forswear allegiance to Mussolini. But even the best-intentioned white men of that time had difficulty thinking of people of the yellow race as Americans.

That is difficult for many people to do even today. Throughout my life, even while I worked as reporter for an American newspaper, I have been asked where I was from.

The questionnaire for issei was changed so that they were asked only to abide by the laws of the United States and not inter-fere with U.S. war efforts. When the issei were further assured that there would not be another forced resettlement while the war continued, more than ninety percent of them answered "yes" to the loyalty questions. As for nisei, a "yes" answer made them sub-ject to the draft and they had more reason than their alien parents to be resentful about how they were being treated. Nevertheless, more than three-quarters of them did pledge their allegiance to The United States. Many of them volunteered for the Army or were drafted and were assigned to the all-nisei 442nd Regimen-tal Combat Team. Fighting in Europe, the 442nd and the 100th Battalion—another all-nisei unit made up mainly of men from Hawaii—were among the most decorated and bloodied units of the war. Thousands of other Japanese Americans, including many kibei, served in the Pacific theater as interpreters and translators and were credited with having given U.S. military intelligence an important advantage over the enemy.

I have compassion today for those nisei who answered "no" to the two critical loyalty questions. They were branded as "no-no boys" and viewed as traitors by some of the more zealous pro-American nisei. Some, mainly Japanese-educated kibei were openly pro-Japan, but others answered "no" because they could not overcome their sense of betrayal and their resentment over how they were being treated by their government. One embittered World War I veteran renounced his U.S. citizenship, saying he wanted to become "a jap a hundred percent." Others wanted to give conditional answers, such as, "Yes, if my rights as a citizen are restored," or "No, not unless the government recognizes my right to live anywhere in the United States," but the government would only accept unconditional pledges of allegiance and loyalty.

Some answered "no" out of a sense of duty to their parents. Filial piety was stressed in every Japanese family. Who would look after their aging parents and younger siblings if left alone in a hostile world?

At Gila there was a family from Guadalupe with six sons, three of them of draft age. At Guadalupe they had lived isolated on a farm far in the country. The family was different from ours, more old-fashioned and "countryish." The parents were fiercely loyal Japanese, not because they were any more patriotic than my parents, but because all their basic relationships were more intense. Even by Japanese standards they were an extremely close-knit family. I could not imagine any of them taking a course of action that would have separated them from their parents or from each other. All of them answered "no" to the loyalty questions. Many years after the war, I visited the family at their farm in California, but we did not talk about Gila. I was doing research on Japanese in the United States and I would have liked to have asked them why they answered "no." But I could not get myself to intrude on their privacy, and besides I already knew the reasons. They answered "no" because they could not repudiate their parents who were loyal Japanese. Whatever fate was in store for them, they would endure it together. From Gila, the family was sent to a camp at Tule Lake, California, which was designated as the camp for "disloyals." At some camps "loyal" nisei, many of them preparing to be inducted into the Army, taunted the deportees saying such things as, "Go on, you dirty japs. We'll kill you the next time we see you."

My brother Nimashi, like my brother-in-law, ended up answering "yes" to the loyalty questions. When I asked Nimashi years later why, he said, "Because I didn't want to go to Tule Lake." At the time, many people thought that those who were sent to Tule Lake would be deported to Japan after the war. Some were.

Many nisei, especially the super patriots, assumed at the time that all or most kibei were anti-American and pro-Japan. It was not as simple as that. Nimashi, who in many ways was a typical kibei, saw much that was attractive about America and the American way of life. But his English was not fluent. The nisei could dream of one day being accepted as Americans, but the kibei saw themselves as permanent outsiders. Nimashi's hero was not John Wayne or James Stewart, it was George Raft, the quintessential anti-hero, and James Cagney in his gangster roles, who operated outside the pale of society. It was infinitely more difficult for a kibei to say yes to America and no to Japan, when in his heart he knew that America did not want him and probably never would.

In 1982, while working on a magazine article about the Japanese in the United States, I interviewed a researcher on the staff of the U.S. Commission on Wartime Relocation and Internment of Civilians, which was created by Congress to reexamine the forced relocation of Japanese and Aleuts during World War II. In the course of our talk, I mentioned that my brother Nimashi was arrested at Gila for joining what authorities thought was a pro-Japanese organization and sent to a special detention camp in Utah. Whereupon, the researcher took out a slim, official-looking volume from the shelf, and asked, "What was your brother's name? Nimashi? Let's see…Here's an entry… Oishi, Nimashi, granted leave to visit family…" I didn't hear much more than that; I was stunned. My brother's name was being read out of government records that had been kept in the 1940s at a World War II detention camp. When I didn't show any interest, the researcher changed the subject and began talking about other matters. I thought I was getting sick and tried to find an excuse for breaking off the interview and leaving when suddenly I began to cry. The researcher, a kindly sympathetic woman, did not seem at all alarmed. "That's all right," she said. "It happens all the time." She walked to the door and closed it, returned to her desk and continued chatting until I was able to regain control of myself. Such a thing had never happened to me before, and I was embarrassed about my momentary breakdown. But it was also good to know, even forty years later, that I was emotionally affected by the arrest of my brother and the tension that surrounded it. I began to see that the most important aspect of my research was not the knowledge and understanding I gained about the incarceration, but my emotional reaction to it. I could finally shed those tears that I could not shed as a child.

7

Soon after we arrived at Gila, our family began to petition the government to "parole" Papa, who was being held in an Army camp in Missoula, Montana. Every member of the family wrote a personal letter and I was also told to write one, which I did without enthusiasm. My family was upset with me. "Don't you want Papa back with us?" they asked. "Sure, I do," I said. But I was lying. My father, in my eyes, had been a huge and powerful presence. The whole family, perhaps even the whole world, trembled before him. Yet, when the war started, he was plucked out of our house by two FBI agents like a feather. I did not want to see him again.

My father was finally "paroled" around the middle of the second year of our incarceration and he was allowed to join us at Gila. He was much changed, quieter and less temperamental. He was sixty years old and for the first time he struck me as an old man. He occupied his time playing go, a Japanese board game, and practicing joruri. From time to time some women in our block would come to our compartment and my father would chant a tragic story of noble sacrifice. While he performed the ladies would take out their handkerchiefs and dab their eyes.

By the time my father joined us at Gila, the political controversy had died down. Most of the young activists were gone, to
the Army, to jobs on the outside, and, in the case of the "troublemakers," to other detention camps. That was no doubt the reason
the authorities allowed my father and other former community
leaders to rejoin their families. It was mainly children and old
folks who remained and life became quiet and settled. There were
kabuki performances, go tournaments, and art exhibits, mainly
of ironwood sculptures. The children played baseball and football
and explored the desert.

I had expected the desert to be hot and dry so I wondered when
we first got to Gila why there were oil heaters in every compartment. With the onset of winter, the reason for them became
clear. At night, it got freezing cold and the windows were misted
with frost in the morning. It did not rain often, but when it did,
it rained as I had never seen before. Storm clouds rolled in quickly
with thunder and lightning that left a sooty smell in the air. Then
the rain would come pouring down. It did not start with a few
sprinkles and grow slowly as it did in Guadalupe, but fell immediately in torrents. Once I was caught in the middle of a firebreak
when it started to rain and suddenly I was knee-deep in water. The
field looked like a churning lake. Unable to see the ground below
me, I stepped into a trench and found myself up to my chest in
water. I finally made it back to our barrack, feeling rather proud of
myself.

The desert was like that, a little scary but challenging. It made
you feel you accomplished something when you learned to get
around in it. Once we got used to our surroundings, my friends
and I went exploring. We flushed brightly colored desert birds out
of the brush, caught horned toads, swam in the irrigation canal,
and climbed the buttes. Some of the older boys went into the desert in the early evening to hunt rattlesnakes for fun. Sometimes
one of them would come back holding the head of a diamondback

that was wrapped around his arm. You could hear the buzzing sound made by the rattles from one end of the block to the other.

It was my brother Goro who first took me out into the desert. We often climbed to top of one of the buttes in the evening to watch the sunset. Gora was 22, twelve years older than I, but we had some wonderful talks. Goro was quiet and the most bookish of my brothers and sisters. He was shy with adults, but he loved to talk and play games with children. In one game we played, I pretended I was playing "I Dream of Jeannie with the Light Brown Hair" on a violin and Goro would clutch his heart and pretend he was in ecstasy, saying, "Oh, oh, I can't stand it." But he could be serious, too. Once, while sitting on top of the butte, he explained to me why the people in China were not upside down, and his explanation helped me understand gravity as I never had before. Gravity pulls us toward the center of the earth, he said. That, for us, is "down." And we experience the opposite direction as "up."

He would also try some of his social theories on me. Christianity, he once told me, was really not a religion in America; it was more a form of social interaction. The teachings of Jesus, he said, were followed only when they conformed to social needs. When I repeated this theory as best I could to Yoshiro, he laughed and said, "That Goro, he's a crazy guy."

We lived close to the edge of camp and the block directly behind us was empty. In one of the barracks were piles of books, mainly used textbooks donated by various groups on the outside. My friends and I would climb through a window of the locked barrack to browse. Most of the books were Dick and Jane type readers and were of little interest. But I did find one volume called *The Golden Treasury of Verse*. I took the book back to the compartment and showed it to Goro, who was delighted with my prize. We read many of the poems together. Goro particularly liked "Annabel Lee" by Edgar Allan Poe, which he recited with great feeling. Then I would recite it and Goro would clutch his heart just as he did when I pretended to play a violin. We also read "The Village Blacksmith" by Henry Wadsworth Longfellow and "O Captain! My Captain!" by Walt Whitman. The three poems remained my favorites and I read them over and over again after Goro left. They sounded like faraway voices calling me.

In college I majored in literature and read a lot of poetry, but I never again developed a relationship with a poem as I did in Gila with my brother and that stolen book. When I read those poems today, it is clear that what appealed to me was the sense of loss they conveyed: a lost love, a lost father, a lost way of life. The poem I understood least well, but which thrilled me the most was Whitman's. It spoke of "My Captain" who is also "My father," a conquering hero, who, having completed a fearful mission, lies on the deck of his ship, "fallen cold and dead." I mourned this fallen man secretly and it seemed to give me some comfort. I wondered uneasily whether the good feeling this poem gave me meant I wanted my own father dead. I was vaguely disappointed when I figured out years later that poem was about the assassination of Lincoln.

The camp school was housed in barracks and had a faculty that was about equally divided between whites and Japanese. The principal at the elementary school was Mr. Strickland, a tall, gaunt man with thinning brown hair and an eagle nose. One day he came into our fifth-grade class to lead us in singing and before he left he taught us this song:

> I ain't got no use for the women,
> A true one is seldom to be found,
> They'll use a man for his money,
> When he's flat they'll turn him down.
>
> They're all alike at the bottom,
> Selfish and grasping for all,
> They'll stay by a man while he's winning,
> And laugh at this face at his fall.

Mr. Strickland came to our class a couple of more times to lead us in singing, and each time we also sang "I ain't got no use for women." The girls, of course, didn't like it, and even the boys thought it was a strange song to sing in school, but Mr. Strickland sang it with gusto and waved his long arms like a symphonic conductor as he led the class in singing it. I don't know whether there was a Mrs. Strickland, but in later years when I thought about Gila and Mr. Strickland I imagined that he was a man whose heart had been broken and who had gone to Gila to escape his sorrows, just as some men might join the French Foreign Legion.

Mr. Strickland, despite his disdain for women, was a kind and outgoing man who seemed to have a genuine liking for us. Around the second year at Gila a school mess hall was opened where we children had lunch. The food there was better than what we got at our block mess hall and we were given second helpings, which we ate like stolen bread, for nobody in any of the other mess halls got second helpings. Once a week there was even ice cream, made with cream, sugar, and dry ice, that Mr. Strickland somehow provided. I assumed that the school mess hall was Mr. Strickland's doing, too, for he made it a point to eat with us, unlike the other white teachers who went to their quarters for lunch.

My school days in Gila were happy ones, but there was one bitter moment. The physical education teacher, a young nisei man, had organized us into a Cub Scout troop and he was going to take us to a boys' camp at Prescott, which was in a wooded area to the north of us. We looked forward to the trip for days, but it was cancelled because the people in Prescott did not want Japanese children there. We had nearly forgotten why we were at Gila in the first place. We had begun to think that we were like everybody else, playing football, having track meets, joining the Cub Scouts. With the cancellation of the Prescott trip we were confronted again with the reality of our situation. We grumbled among ourselves about it, saying things like, "Hakujin people are dumb," and "Hakujin people really hate us."

Long after the war, I learned that among the white people in the camps were anthropologists who were sent to study the Japanese so that the government would have better insight into the enemy mentality. Some of them, and perhaps other white people, too, brought their families along. There was one white boy at Gila who came to school wearing a hunting knife on his belt. We Japanese children assumed he wore it to protect himself from us. His family either left Gila or the boy was sent away because he stopped coming to school after the first year. We were glad to be rid of him. He and his knife were a constant reminder of what some white people thought of us.

When my father, my mother, and I were the only ones left of our family at Gila, we were allowed to transfer to Poston where my sister Hiroko and her family were. The desert surrounding Poston was not nearly as beautiful as Gila. Unlike Gila with its red and white barracks, Poston had the same smelly tar-papered barracks as the other camps. The people had planted castor and other bushes and flowers, but none of that could overcome the oppressive ugliness of the black, smutty tar paper.

The Colorado River was seven miles away, but by the time I got to Poston must of the children had already been there several times and did not want to make the long hike again. They said the river was dangerous, with strong undercurrents, and one boy had drowned swimming in it. But the main reason why the river was not as attractive as it might have been was the swimming pool. It was actually a small reservoir the people had made by digging an L-shaped hole in the ground and diverting water to it from an irrigation canal. It had high and low diving boards, wooden railings, and a rough-hewn pavilion with benches for people who wanted to just sit and watch. During my two summers in Poston, every day was spent at the pool where we dove for pennies, played tag, and even wrestled in deep water.

Food was served "family style" at Poston. Each family was assigned a table and the food was brought to the tables by girls serving as waitresses, so there was no standing in line. My mother got a job as a dishwasher, for which she was paid $16 a month. I don't think the amount made much of a difference to her. She simply liked the idea of getting paid for her work. When she got her first paycheck, she said, "I don't want to cash it. I want to keep it forever. I've been working all my life and this is the first time anybody has paid me." Working in the mess hall had other benefits. From time to time she brought home leftover milk, bread, and apple butter. The milk soured quickly in the heat and it made me a little nauseous but I drank it anyway. In Poston I gained back the weight I had lost at Gila.

Goro, after he finished his basic training, came to visit us at Poston. He looked good in his Army uniform and a lot stronger. We went on walks by the irrigation canal and he would tell me about Camp Shelby. "You know, in Mississippi," he said, "if you talk to a Negro guy, a hakujin will come and slap you on the shoulder and say, 'Hey, don't talk to those guys.'" Goro used swear words, something he had never done before. About the strongest expression he used before he went into the Army was "holy mackerel," but now he peppered his talk with "goddamn" and "son-of-a-bitch." Once, while we were on a walk, Goro said, "You know, it's kids like you who are suffering the most from this experience. You have to spend your formative years in a camp in the desert. For Yosh and me it doesn't matter that much. Our characters are already formed, but you, you're missing a lot. If I were you, I'd sue the goddamn government for a million dollars after the war."

Goro is known as "the joker" in the family because he was always saying amusing things in his quiet way. I thought he might be making another one of his jokes, but he was very serious. After he left, I thought about what he said, especially the words, "formative years," which sounded deep and full of complicated meaning. Long after the war I asked Goro if he remembered telling me those things and he laughed and said he had no recollection of it.

In Poston, I was twelve years old, in the third year of incarceration, and Goro made me think more about what the government had done to us. I memorized the Gettysburg Address, in part for the fun of it because I remembered Goro going around the house in Guadalupe, with his chest out, saying very solemnly, "Four score and seven years ago..." But I memorized it mainly because I liked the words. I did not understand some parts of it, but I could understand the founding of "a new nation, conceived in liberty and dedicated to the proposition that all men are created equal." When I told Mrs. Evans, our sixth-grade teacher, that I knew the Gettysburg Address by heart, she had me recite it in front of the class.

Several weeks later, when President Roosevelt died, Mrs. Evans asked me to recite the Gettysburg Address at a special memorial service we were having at the school. I agreed to do it, but as the time for the service approached I became increasingly troubled by the idea. I could not see any connection between what Lincoln said during the Civil War and President Roosevelt's death. I went to Mrs. Evans to tell her I didn't want to recite the Gettysburg Address because it did not make any sense at a service for President Roosevelt. Mrs. Evans argued that it did, but could not persuade me to change my mind.

At the service the children from both the elementary and high school gathered outside with each class standing together in rows as in a military formation. As I listened to the speeches I was glad I was not taking part in the ceremonies. It made me uncomfortable to hear Japanese students delivering eulogies. President Roosevelt might have been a great man and a great president, but he was the one who had put us in the camp. I experienced no sorrow at his death; I felt no emotion whatsoever.

When the war ended, Poston began gradually to empty. In the block next to ours a family of Hopi Indians moved into one of the barracks. They had chickens and a pair of goats in a makeshift pen made of chicken wire. They were very friendly people and allowed us children to pat the goats. One of my friends took the teat of the she-goat and squirted milk at me. I thought the owners would be upset, but they only laughed. The grandfather of the family liked to talk to us and he told us how the white man had taken their land away. One day, he said, there would be a great Indian uprising and they would take all the land back. Later, other Indian families began to move into the camp and sometimes late at night you could hear an Indian brave shouting what might have been a war chant at the top of his lungs. It seems eerie when I think back on our final days in Poston, on a community of imprisoned Japanese beginning to scatter, the barracks taking on a look of deterioration as the desert reasserted its claim, and the Hopi Indians, the true owners of the land, gathering slowly, prophesying war. Toward the end of our stay I thought I could hear coyotes howling at night.

The government began a resettlement program and helped my brother-in-law Nobuo get a job in Los Angeles as a truck driver for a paint company. After several weeks, he was able to rent an apartment in a housing project in nearby Long Beach where the rest of us joined him. And so, in late summer of 1945, after three years of incarceration, we were freed.

8

We spent one year in Long Beach after the war, and returned to
Guadalupe in the summer of 1946. A few Japanese families had
returned, but not many. There was a new bowling alley on Main
Street, but Guadalupe looked poorer than it had before and quieter. There were five of us, Papa, Mama, Yoshiro and his wife Suek,
and me. Yoshiro and Suek had got married in Minnesota where he
had been sent by the Army to study Japanese at a military intelligence school. Suek bad been a Japanese language instructor there.
We came into town in a 1936 Buick Yoshiro had bought, hauling a
small trailer that held all our belongings. Nobody took any notice
of us when we pulled up in front of our old store. There were reports that in some places where Japanese had returned guns were
fired into their homes, but nobody bothered us.

There was a peculiar smell and when we got to the room that
connected the storefront with the living quarters and we saw there
was a dead kitten on the floor covered with maggots. Another
kitten, looking half starved, came out of the living room mewing
piteously. The ceiling was draped with heavy layers of cobweb and

the walls were thick with grease and grime. A Mexican family had lived there for a while and after they left vagrants apparently used to break in to spend the night in the house. In the bathroom there were crusty remains of human or animal feces and pieces of used, dirty toilet paper stuffed under the bathtub.

I wondered whether we were actually going to stay in this house. I would have liked to have gotten back into the car and driven back to Long Beach, but Papa started ordering us around and it was clear we were spending the night there. I was given the task of getting rid of the dead kitten and nearly threw up getting the stinking, maggot-covered carcass in a brown paper bag. I took it out to the backyard and lit a match to the bag and watched the maggots shrivel up in the flames. When I went back into the house the trailer was already unloaded and Mama and Suek were cleaning out the kitchen, which was covered with dirty grease and rat droppings. Somebody, probably Yoshiro, had seen to it that the utilities were turned on because we had electricity and water and the gas stove worked. While Mama cooked, we cleaned out three of the rooms in which we were to sleep. As we knocked down the cobwebs and swept out the house, I could smell the rice steaming in the kitchen and what seemed like an unbearable situation gradually became bearable. It took, however, a week of steady work by the five of us before the house was in a condition where we didn't have to walk around with our shoulders hunched to avoid touching the walls.

The rats had multiplied in our absence and had got brazen as if they were now the owners of the house and we were the intruders. Instead of scurrying away when they saw us they would stand their ground and stare until we made a menacing gesture. We trapped and killed a great many rats in the first weeks, huge ones that refused to die even when their skulls were crushed. We chased one wounded rat in the hallway and as my mother and I blocked its escape with a large sheet of plywood, my father entered with a broom. He pinned the rat against the wall with the broom, then crushed it with his foot. As he did so, he twirled the broom like a spear and with the classic head movements of a Kabuki actor, shouted, "Akechi Mitsuhide!!!!" the climactic line of one his favorite plays. We laughed. It was a happy moment.

Yoshiro and Suek didn't stay long in Guadalupe. After a week they returned to Long Beach where Yoshiro joined Nobuo in a vegetable peddling business. I could not believe that they would abandon us and was bitter about it. That night, after Yoshiro and Suek left, I lay in bed feeling utterly miserable and lonely. There was nobody left, it seemed. Nimashi had settled in Phoenix with his wife. Goro was in Japan with the occupation troops and Hoshiko was away at college. As I lay in bed, I could hear the rats scurrying back and forth in the ceiling over my head. The mattress had a clean sheet over it, but it still gave off a musty smell. Under the sheet there were large blotches made by some stranger's vomit or urine. The wind was howling as it often did in Guadalupe at night and it came through the cracks in the wall. I could hear the murmur of my parents talking in the next room, but it gave me little comfort. Instead, it only added to my loneliness. I was thirteen years old at the time, about the age when a boy becomes a man in some cultures. In the Japanese culture, the age of passage is sixteen, but I think my childhood ended that night as I lay in the dark crying, furious at life and at the world.

My father bought a 1936 Ford for $700. That was about all the money we had, but he needed a car if he and Mama were going to find work. My father had lost everything except the house. His farms had been leased, so we no longer had them. The farm equipment had either been sold for a pittance or simply abandoned. The crops had been left for somebody else to harvest and we were never paid for them.

My father, who was 62 when we returned to Guadalupe after the war, had not done any field work since he was 20 years old. My mother was 53 and had never been in the fields. So they had difficulty getting on a work crew. Mr. Uno, one of Nimashi's kibei friends, was working as a labor contractor and had promised to put my parents on his crew, but he did not do so for some time. He probably had some misgivings about hiring such aging and inexperienced workers. For days, my parents grumbled about Mr. Uno, letting slip from time to time some unkind thoughts about a man whose sudden rise in the world as a labor contractor would cause him to forget past favors and obligations Finally, Mr. Uno found a job drying nasturtium plants for seeds that the two of them could do. I went on two weekends to help them. After my parents proved themselves as good workers on that job, they were put on the regular crew, but they always reminisced about the nasturtium job. "That was a good job," they would say. "If only we could get another job like that."

When I turned sixteen I was also allowed to work in the fields during summer vacations. The hardest work was thinning lettuce, which was done standing, bent at the waist with short-handled hoes. My parents at their age could not hoe a long row bending from the waist, so they did it squatting, shuffling along on their knees. Until you got used to the work, you went limping off the field at the end of the day with your muscles cramped und aching. My parents never got used to it. On their days off they moved slowly and carefully as if they were afraid they would break a bone. The work aggravated my father's rheumatism so my mother was always applying medicated plasters to his back to ease the pain.

The pay was seventy-five cents an hour and we worked ten hours a day, six days a week. Besides thinning lettuce, we bunched carrots, harvested celery, picked tomatoes and strawberries, and cut flowers. Some of it was piecework, which my parents preferred because they did not feel as much pressure to keep pace with the others. The crew we worked on consisted mostly of Japanese, including men and women in their fifties who had been farm laborers all their lives. The women were rough in their language and manners. They made crude sexual jokes and laughed raucously. I would glance sidelong at my mother at those times and was glad to see that she took it in good humor and laughed appreciatively so as not to seem uppity. But she rarely joined in the general conversation and bantering. What was especially difficult for my mother was seeing women not wanting to lose time from piecework just stepping a few rows over, lowering their trousers and relieving themselves in full sight of everyone. At such times I could see her clamp her jaws and stare fiercely into the ground. That these same women would be more delicate about meeting their bodily needs when they were being paid by the hour only heightened their shamelessness in my mother's eyes. "How could they be so greedy," she would say angrily. My father had less difficulty with the crude ways of the women. He conversed freely with them and joined in with their joking. He chatted easily with the Mexicans, too. He would comment on the heat, saying "Muy caliente, huh?" and when the day was over, he would shout, "Vamanos, muchachos, vamanos para casa!" While he worked, I could see his lips moving and I would know that he was practicing his joruri. On his days off he began a project of transcribing those he knew by heart with Japanese brush and ink. He did it slowly with great care and completed volume after volume.

During school days my parents were usually gone by the time I got up and I would find a plate of cold eggs and fried rice or pota-toes on the kitchen table. When I got home from school, I would have the house to myself until six o'clock or so when my parents came home from work. My father wore a pair of patched woolen pants, a flannel shirt, and, over everything, a canvas carpenter's apron that covered the front of his legs. My mother had sewn in padding over the knees, so he looked almost as if he were in armor. My mother wore multi-layers of loose cotton shirts and trousers and a broad straw hat tied firmly on her head with a large white kitchen towel. They made a strange-looking couple. I was usually in my room listening to the afternoon adventure serials on the radio or reading when they came in and I could hear their slow, heavy steps go past my door. The routine was always the same and I knew every moment what my parents were doing without ever leaving my room. My mother would start the bath running, then go to the kitchen to start dinner. Sometimes she would have already made stew or spaghetti in a big pot the night before, so she only needed to take it out of the refrigerator and warm it up. Sometimes she sent me to the Chinese restaurant where, for two dollars, you could get a huge platter piled high with chow mein. While my mother cooked, my father soaked in near-boiling water. He liked his bath water so hot that when he got in he felt stabbed by a thousand needles. My father usually had a beer with supper and before he started to eat he would drink half the glass in one long pull. He would lower the glass, wipe his mouth with the back of his hand, and say, "Aaaaah.... It's the first swallow that's the best. There's nothing like the sensation of cold beer going down your throat when you're thirsty. It's indescribable." It was always the same, word for word.

We no longer had many visitors at the house. Like my father, most of the farmers were not able to reestablish themselves. They never returned to Guadalupe; they lived elsewhere, supported by their children. My mother used to be a member of the Women's Association before the war and she used to have friends drop by for tea now and then, but after the war there was not a single woman in Guadalupe whom she could call a friend.

My parents didn't talk about the shift in their fortunes. I could see they were tired and sore from their field work, but they didn't complain and made no special demands on me. The main change that I saw was a greater intimacy between my father and mother. They talked to each other in soft whispers as I had never seen them do before the war. My mother stopped criticizing her husband behind his back. When she talked of him it was in a sympathetic tone. My father, in his turn, didn't shout at her anymore. Sometimes he would ask her if she was tired and offer to do the cooking.

My father still had outbursts of temper, but it was usually

directed at me, usually for not being prompt enough in obeying his commands. His moods were worst in winter when there were long periods without work and he would go off and drink and play cards. There was one stretch when he didn't come home for three days and my mother went around silently with a furrowed brow, keeping her thoughts to herself.

My father's favorite joruri, which he practiced endlessly in those days, was the story of a faithful vassal who is hiding and protecting the son and heir of his vanquished lord. The conquering lord, anxious to eliminate all potential pretenders to the throne, sends out his lieutenants to hunt down the young prince. When the boy is finally located, the guardian is ordered to bring in the head of his charge. The vassal, still faithful to his dead lord, kills his own son instead. The samurai who is charged with identifying the head sees immediately that it is not that of the young prince. He understands in an instant what has taken place and is so filled with admiration for the faithful vassal that he falsely identifies the head as belonging to the prince.

This theme of steadfast loyalty contrasted sharply with my father's attitude towards the outcome of the war. He carried around in his wallet photographs of my two brothers in combat gear taken at Camp Shelby, Mississippi. When my father went to the bank, post office, or to some white store, he would fumble with his wallet until the pictures fell out. Then he would show them to the clerk. "My boys," he would say, "fight in American Army." I cringed every time I saw him do that. First of all, my brothers never saw combat. After basic training they were sent to a military intelligence school to be trained as Japanese translators and interpreters. But even if they had, my father would have been opposed to their fighting in the American Army. I knew my father thought of hakujin as children, as people one had to humor. He was employing the art of survival he had cultivated over the decades as an unwanted immigrant in America. Even so, I saw his performance as hypocrisy, as groveling. I would have been prouder of him if he had said something outrageous like, "You cowardly Americans. We Japanese will conquer you yet."

My father's interest in Japanese history remained strong after the war and he continued to tell historical stories. One story he told was about a famous thief by the name of Ishikawa Goemon, who, to show off his skill, steals a valuable scroll belonging to the great lord Toyotomi Hideyoshi. Goemon is eventually caught and, to make an example of him, Hideyoshi condemns not only him, but also his wife and children to be boiled in oil. At the execution, when the oil begins to heat up, Goemon grabs his two young sons and holds their heads under the oil to spare them a slow, agonizing death. In my imagination I saw Goemon glaring at his executioners, defiant to the end.

My father, it seemed to me, was condemned by his own stories. His behavior before hakujin by contrast was weak and unmanly. It made the imperious tone he took with me from time to time all the more difficult to bear. I raged inwardly over his lording it over me. I couldn't stand listening to his fatherly admonitions. His foibles, his every show of weakness, infuriated me, but I was still afraid of him and did not dare confront him directly. As my mother did before the war, I grumbled behind his back and on one occasion— I no longer remember what it was that made me so angry— I shouted at my mother, "I hate him! I hate Papa!" I was instantly sorry for having said that, for my mother looked as if I had pierced her heart with a knife. "Don't say that," she pleaded. "Don't say such a thing. Don't you see what has happened to him? Don't you feel any pity for him? And on top of everything, to be hated by his own son. No, don't say such a thing. It's too cruel." The word my mother used to describe her husband was "kawaiso," a word full of compassion. There is no English equivalent. It means pitiful or pathetic but without the contemptuous tone of these English words. It is a word one might use to describe a child who has been left an orphan. Or, for that matter, it is a word one might use to describe a man who has lost everything he had striven for all his life and is reduced to working as a common laborer in his old age while his youngest son, on whom he dotes, curses him behind his back.

I can understand today why my mother reacted as she did, but at the time it was impossible for me to see my father as "kawaiso." Even as a field laborer, he was, in my eyes, still a godlike figure and one does not feel pity for a god. I knew my father cared about me. Perhaps his story about Ishikawa Goemon was his way of reminding me of a father's natural instincts and love for his children, no matter in what a gruesome way they can be expressed. My father worried about my future and he was pleased that I did well in school. I knew he loved me and was proud of me, but I could not return his love.

In 1960, when I was 27 years old, I accompanied my parents on a trip to Japan. There, one night at a hotel, my father and I shared a beer. In the Japanese fashion, he filled my glass and I filled his. We didn't say much. We only raised our glasses to one another. For the first time in my life I was not afraid in his presence and I felt that we could have been friends. The moment passed quickly, but I cherish it in my memory because it was the closest I ever got to friendship with my father.

9

One of the first people I recognized in Guadalupe was a former classmate, a Portuguese boy named Norman. We had started kindergarten together, and even though I could speak little English at the time, we had become friends. Later I even went to his house to play. Norman had grown considerably taller in the intervening four years, but I recognized him instantly. "Hi, Norman," I said. "Remember me? I'm Gene." I waited for a smile of recognition, but Norman just stood there with his head tilted back, eyeing me up and down. Then, finally, he said, "All you japs coming back?"

When school started, it became even clearer that Norman and I were no longer friends. He tormented me throughout the eighth grade with remarks about my race. What seemed to offend him most was the shape of my nose. "You guys all have flat faces," he would say. "And you got skinny arms. God, I hate your skinny arms."

When a new teacher, an ex-Marine officer, came to the school, Norman, in my presence, asked him in a loud voice, "Mr. M, how many japs did you kill?" When the teacher did not respond, I chimed in, "Yeah, Mr. M., how many japs did you kill?" I wanted to show that Norman's question had nothing to do with me, but the teacher looked at me with a quizzical expression and continued to ignore the question.

When we went to high school the following year, Norman and I were on different academic tracks, so we only had physical education together. During swimming he began coming up behind me and dunking me every chance he got. One day, when he tried to dunk me in the deepest part of the pool, I turned on him and held him under the water. I was surprised at how weak of an underwater wrestler he was. I came perilously close to drowning him. When I let him up, he thrashed his way to the edge of the pool, clambered out, and stood there hunched over like a wet alley cat. He never said another word to me again.

My only friend during that first year back in Guadalupe was Ronald, the son of Mrs. Brunner, the second-grade teacher who had taken Miss Kennedy's place. Ronald sought me out and after we became friends, he said, "My mother says you're the type of boy I should associate with." He then looked at me as if he were waiting for me to contradict his mother.

There weren't many middle-class white families living in Guadalupe at the time. Most of them had moved to Santa Maria, which was only ten miles away. The white children going to school in Guadalupe were now mainly from working-class families. The older ones, those who were marking time in grammar school until they were sixteen and could drop out, smoked cigarettes and talked about fucking girls in the back of old jalopies. Some of the white girls in the eighth grade already had large breasts and wore makeup. One girl named Bernice wore low-cut blouses, tight skirts and slacks, and open-toed shoes. Sometimes during lunch, when the teacher was not there, she would sit on a desk at the front of the class with her legs crossed, take out her compact, and powder her face. She looked like a movie star. Ronald got very excited when he saw her do that. "Gosh, she's so beautiful," he said. "I'd sure like to fuck her. Wouldn't you, Gene?" I thought, too, that Bernice was beautiful and desirable, but I never admitted it. She was the kind of hakujin girl that my parents disapproved of. They would have said that all that lipstick and makeup indicated a bad family and a bad character. "I don't think she's so pretty," I told Ronald.

After school, Ronald and I would go to my house because my parents usually weren't home and we had the house to ourselves. The first time Ronald came to our house, he said, "This isn't a slum, huh, Gene?" and looked at me for confirmation. It seemed to be an honest question, it wasn't a sly way of insulting me, but it upset me. Ronald often had cigarettes and he would want to smoke in the house, but I wouldn't let him. "You can't smoke in your own house, so you can't smoke in mine," I told him.

Ronald belonged to a Masonic boy's club in Santa Maria. He used to tell me what a great time he had at club meetings so I asked him whether I could join. "Naw," he said without a moment's hesitation, "it's only for good guys." When we started to go to high school in Santa Maria, Ronald began to distance himself from me. Santa Maria was only a fifteen-minute bus ride from Guadalupe, but it was a world apart. Santa Maria was where white people lived with fine houses on streets lined with trees and lawns, where there were fashionable stores, three movie theaters, a traffic light, a Rotary Club, and a Presbyterian church. Santa Maria was middle America where freckled kids like Mickey Rooney in the old Andy Hardy movies lived and said things like, "Gosh, Mom," and "Gee whiz, Dad." The student body at the high school was predominantly white and all the popular students were middle class. The boys wore denims and sport shirts and had short haircuts; the girls looked wholesome, wore sweaters, skirts, bobby sox, and brown shoes. Many of the students from Guadalupe Grammar School never made it to high school and those who did were not part of the social mainstream. Ronald, who had been so taken with Bernice in Guadalupe, was surprised that she did not look so attractive in the Santa Maria setting. "She looks like nothing now," he said. "I told you," I said. In truth, Bernice didn't look as glamorous as she had at the Guadalupe grammar school; she was dowdy in clothes that now looked like hand-me-downs. But I still thought she was pretty and when I saw her walking alone and looking lonely, I liked her a lot more than I had in Guadalupe, where she had been the most popular girl in class and totally unapproachable. When I passed her I would say "Hi," or nod to her and she would say "Hi," and smile.

The Brunners moved to Santa Maria when Ronald and I were sophomores, so he no longer had to ride the bus every day to school and we became like strangers. When we passed in the halls, he ignored me. I got the feeling that he was angry at me, as he was at Bernice, for having deceived him in some way. He should not have been. He had known all along that I was not one of the "good guys."

I was lonely in high school, but my biggest concern was not my loneliness but looking lonely. I didn't want to be like Bernice going from class to class alone and having no one to talk to. There were some Japanese students, but I associated with them only at Guadalupe where I attended dances they held. I did not hang out with them at school. They thought I was "stuck-up" and considered myself too good for them, but that was not the reason I didn't associate with them in Santa Maria. It made me extremely uncomfortable to see Japanese students walking together from class to class. I didn't see any safety in clinging together. To the contrary, it seemed to me that the most foolish thing Japanese could do was to flock together, for it made us more noticeable. It was better to merge with the surroundings, to become inconspicuous, to be like everybody else. I worked hard at cultivating friendships with whites—boys who were college bound and much admired by the teachers. I had a measure of success, but the friendships I made were superficial. I ate lunch with a group of white boys, walked from class to class with them, and sat with them during school assemblies, but I never saw them after school or on weekends.

Once, a boy named Danny, a tall, good-looking student with a sunny disposition, invited me to attend his church. It was a Presbyterian Church and the congregation was entirely white. After the service, Danny invited me to his home for lunch. It was a Tudor half-timbered house, which I had often seen from the outside. It was not any more impressive than the other houses on the block, but to me it was a mansion, the sort of place one can observe from the outside, but not from within. I was overwhelmed when I entered, for except in movies and in magazines, I had never seen such affluence. There was a sunken living room with an expansive hardwood floor. There were plush sofas and chairs, pictures on the walls, vases on the tables, and a grand piano. Most impressive of all was the house itself. It was solid and not one that rats could gnaw through or that would sway in the wind. Danny's mother, who had not been at the service, was not overly warm in her welcome. Danny had not told her he was bringing me home for lunch. There was a whispered conversation between him and his mother in the kitchen and it turned out that I was not staying for lunch after all.

There were a few white girls with whom I chatted and joked around with at school, but those relationships were fraught with dangers. Neither my parents nor theirs would have approved, nor the white community or the Japanese, whatever was left of it. Once, in the ninth-grade civics class, before class began, the students at my table began discussing interracial marriage. I kept myself out of the discussion, but at one point, Lenore, a red-haired girl with whom I was particularly friendly, said, "I happen to like a boy of another race." She looked directly at me as she said it. I pretended I didn't hear. My immediate reaction was jealousy and I wondered why a nice girl like Lenore would be fooling around with a boy of another race. Eventually, I began to wonder whether I was the one Lenore liked and was tortured by the thought, for if it were me, there was nothing I could do. My parents would have been devastated if they thought I liked a hakujin girl, and I had no doubt that Lenore's parents would have been equally appalled. Once, when I was late leaving the civics class, Lenore was still there and said, "Well, I guess you're going to have to walk me to our next class." As we walked together a group of Japanese students passed us and I thought I saw contempt in their faces. I, who was too good for them, now had a hakujin girlfriend. White students glanced at us, too. After that I bolted out of the civics class so I would not be caught alone with Lenore.

From all outward appearances I was a happy and contented boy in high school. I was an honor student. My teachers liked me and my fellow students accepted me. While still at Guadalupe Grammar School, I had learned to play the trombone on a school instrument, and when I went to high school, my parents bought me a used trombone for $42 so I could play in the school band. I would have gone out for the football team, too, but my parents would not sign the consent form, saying it was too dangerous. When I argued that they could not know it was dangerous since they had never seen a football game, my father attended the next game. He was shocked. "No. Never," he said. "I'll never let you play that game." When we got home, he told my mother, "They just knock each other down. They run as fast they can and knock each other down." My mother nodded her head and agreed that football was much too dangerous a game for me to play. I was furious. After that, I blamed my parents for my unhappiness, for if I could have played on the varsity football team, I could have been part of the school and felt that I belonged.

I spent much of my free time listening to the radio and reading. In our bookcase there were some novels that my brothers had bought in college. Among them was *Arrowsmith* by Sinclair Lewis. I was intrigued by the name—I thought it was going to be about Indians—so I read it. I had read adventure books before, books like *Treasure Island* and *Kidnapped*, but *Arrowsmith* was the first book I read that seemed to be about real people. Martin Arrowsmith, it seemed to me, was the first hakujin I got to know well. While I was reading the book, he seemed like a friend. I liked his wife, too, and was sad when she died and I was sad when I finished the book. After that I read other books by Sinclair Lewis, then books by Mark Twain, Jack London, Steinbeck, and Hemingway. I judged how good the books were by how sad I was when I finished them.

In my junior year, we read *Our Town* by Thornton Wilder in the English class. Mrs. Gotley asked us to write briefly in class what the play had meant to us. I wrote quickly and petulantly that I could hardly get any impression at all from this strange play which described a family and culture so completely different from my own. I was great embarrassed when Mrs. Gotley, a very spontaneous woman, kneeled next to my desk to sympathize with me in front of the whole class. Although she did not know it, Mrs. Gotley had caught me in a lie. I had understood *Our Town* all too well, but while I could share Wilder's sense of loss, I could not participate in the nostalgia evoked by the play. I would have liked to have been George Gibbs, who did his algebra homework with his girlfriend Emily by whispering from his bedroom window to hers in the house next door. It made me angry to read about his carrying Emily's book and taking her to Mr. Morgan's drugstore to buy her an ice cream soda, when I couldn't even walk down the hall with a girl I liked. But there was no way I could tell Mrs. Gotley about the envy I felt, so I said, "Oh, the play wasn't that different from my childhood. I understood it." Mrs. Gotley, looking perplexed, returned to her desk.

After I started going to high school, music became increasingly important and gradually dominated my life and thoughts. The school band was the one place where I felt accepted and where I felt comfortable. Later I joined the school dance band and played at school dances. I was accepted by the American Legion Band so I rehearsed with them one evening a week and marched in parades in Santa Maria and surrounding communities. With the money I made working in the fields, I bought a used piano and began taking piano lessons.

When I was four or five I had agreed with my mother that I would be a doctor when I grew up, but around the second year of high school, I told her that I had changed my mind and was going to be a musician instead. My mother and my father were both appalled, but seemed to know that it was useless to try to dissuade me. They said it might be very difficult to earn a living as a musician and did not say much more than that. I did not tell them that not only did I want to be a musician, I wanted to be a jazz musician. They would not have understood the distinction and if they had, they would have been even more alarmed.

In our ninth-grade civics class, we were encouraged to start thinking about our future careers, so I started reading books about music. I read a book by Eddie Condon called *We Call It Music*, in which he wrote about jazz, Prohibition, bathtub gin, speakeasies, and some of the more colorful antics of the musicians of his day. From Eddie Condon's book, I got the impression that jazz musicians led unwholesome, dissolute, but irresistibly appealing lives. If you wanted to destroy yourself—and I thought I did—there was no better way to do it than leading a dissipated life: smoking, drinking, staying up until all hours, and playing this exciting, totally absorbing music.

I wanted to do violence to my mind and body. I was convinced there was something wrong with me. I hated being Japanese. It seemed to me that about the meanest thing God—if there really was a God—could do to anybody was to make him Japanese. When one of my music teachers at school told us about the curse on Tchaikovsky's Sixth Symphony, I bought the album. The teacher had said that Tchaikovsky died shortly after he completed the work, and that it was said that whenever it was performed somebody died. Every afternoon, when I was alone in the house, I would draw the shades, put the records on the phonograph, lie on the couch, and wait for the curse to strike. I thought the fourth movement, the Adagio, was boring, but I faithfully listened to it because if the curse lived anywhere it surely resided in that slow and mournful fourth movement. When I remained alive after numerous hearings, I bought the score to see whether I could discover anything by studying the written music. It was the first time I had seen a symphonic score, and I was struck by how every note one heard was accounted for on paper. After that, whenever I listened to the symphony, I followed the music on the score and didn't think much more about the curse.

Studying Tchaikovsky's score made me think that I could write music too, so I ordered a book on arranging I saw advertised in *Downbeat* magazine. From the book, I learned how to transpose music for trumpets and saxophones, a little about voicing, and about the ranges of the different instruments. But I didn't know much about harmony or chord progressions. Nevertheless, I decided to arrange the song "Margie" for our school dance band. I had recently seen a movie, starring Jeanne Crain, with that title and had been moved by it. I arranged the song note by note. I played a note of the melody on the piano and poked around until I found three other notes that sounded right with it. Then I proceeded to the next note and did the same thing. When I got through the entire song that way, I assigned the notes first to the brass section, then to the saxophones. Then using the notes in the chords I had formed, I made up a little obligato. When the brass played the melody, I had the saxophones play the obligato, and vice versa. I took the arrangement to Mr. Henderson, who directed the dance band, and he had the band play it. I had feared that it would be a mess, but it sounded fine. The harmony was okay and even the obligato worked pretty well. Mr. Henderson said it was a fine arrangement and that I should write more. If I had to pick the biggest thrill I have ever had in my life, I would have little difficulty deciding. It was the moment the band started to play my arrangement of "Margie."

In 1950, at the end of my junior year in high school, my brother Yoshiro started a small grocery store in San Pedro and he wanted us to go there to help him run it. As much as I hated Guadalupe, I didn't want to leave. I wanted at least to finish high school in Santa Maria. I was playing in the dance band there and happy with music. Mr. Henderson, when he heard we were moving away, offered to let me stay at his house through my senior year. He said he had talked it over with his wife and she had agreed to it. He thought he could help me with my piano playing and arranging. I wanted to accept the offer, but my parents would not hear of it; they would not even consent to talking with Mr. Henderson about it. And so, feeling misused, I went with my parents to San Pedro to live once more in a small rickety house behind a small rickety store.

10

San Pedro, situated at the mouth of Los Angeles Harbor, still had
the reputation of a tough seaport town in the 1950s, though it was
not as tough as it had been in earlier days. My brother's store was
located across the street from a public housing project in a poor
section of town near the harbor. Beacon Street, where it was said
in the old days that at least one man was killed every night, was
not far from our store. We lived in a small frame house behind the
store. It had a kitchen and three tiny rooms. Yoshiro and Suek had
one bedroom, Mama and Papa the other, and I slept in what was
supposed to be the living room. The store was called Eagle Grocery.
It had been owned by a Mexican man who decided to quit when
business fell off. Yoshiro extended the store's hours to twelve
hours a day, seven days a week, expanded the inventory, got up at
four A.M. twice a week to buy fresh vegetables himself at the Los
Angeles produce market, had regular specials, and held drawings
for free turkeys before Thanksgiving Day and Christmas. Within
a few months, Eagle Grocery, a sleepy shack of a store patronized
by welfare recipients and the working poor, became a thriving

enterprise with a volume of business that equaled that of a small supermarket. Wholesale salesmen were astounded by the quantity of merchandize that moved through this tiny neighborhood store every week.

It was strictly a family operation. Goro, who had come back from Japan with a Japanese bride, could not find a medical school that would accept him, so he went to work for Yoshiro as a butcher. My mother and father went early every morning to clean the vegetables and to stock the produce bins. When they finished, my mother would do housework or spell Suek as cashier. My father puttered around, sweeping up and taking care of empty beer and soft drink bottles. I worked on weekends, stocking the shelves, helping behind the butcher counter, or bagging groceries. After a year, Yoshiro bought a vacant lot near the store and an old frame house, which he had moved onto it. After papering and painting the inside, stuccoing the outside, and hooking up the utilities, my parents and I moved in. It was a modest, two-bedroom bungalow, not as good a house as my mother had long dreamed of, but it was not bad enough so that she could complain about it.

The atmosphere at San Pedro High School was very different from that in Santa Maria. Most of the white students were second or third generation Slavs and many of their names ended with "ich" or "vich." There were also Italians, Mexicans, and a few Filipinos and Blacks. There was one other Japanese boy who was a senior, but we had no classes together and I never got to know him.

The central building of San Pedro High was huge, starkly functional, and ugly. There was a fence around the school and the gates were kept locked during school hours so that you could not leave the grounds even during lunch. Some of the students looked and acted like thugs, though they didn't bother you if you didn't them. Except for Mr. Asher, the band director, I never got to know any of my teachers very well. Compared to Santa Maria, there was no sense of community. San Pedro High School was a big-city, mind-your-own-business kind of place. But I liked it better because I didn't stick out. There were not many of what I could have called normal white people at the school and everybody seemed somehow more equal.

The first trombonist in the San Pedro High School band was a boy named Lester Robertson. The first question he asked me when I took a seat next to him in band practice was, "You dig bop?" I knew about bebop because I had subscribed to *Downbeat* magazine in Guadalupe. And at Santa Maria, Tommy Palmquist, the lead trumpet player in our dance band, used to play what he said were bop riffs. But I had never heard a Charlie Parker or a Dizzy Gillespie record. Even so, I told Lester, "Yeah, man. I dig bop." Lester was pleased. "That's cool, man," he said. Lester and his friends divided the world into two kinds of people, "cats" and "squares," and I knew right off that I wanted to be one of the "cats." And for the first time since I left the internment camp, I had real friends, all members of the band who were interested in jazz. One of the boys was of Slavic ancestry, another Italian, a third Filipino. Lester, who became my best friend, was Black.

When we graduated high school, Lester and I went to Los Angeles City College together. Lester's father was a retired Navy man who supplemented his pension as a part-time salesman. His mother, a big, robust woman, fussed around the house, which she kept immaculately clean and neat, and worried about Lester. They were Roman Catholics and Lester, when he was little, had gone to a Catholic school. We had much in common. We both got our haircuts on time and our mothers made sure that we went to school in clean, well-pressed clothes. Neither of us was much interested in race or ethnicity. But we had something approaching a common ethnicity in music. The world of music had its own values, attitudes, and even language. The conversation between Lester and me often went something like this:

"Man, this is a real drag."

"Yeah, man. I'm hip."

"We ought to get our own pad, man. Wouldn't that be cool? We could jam any time we wanted. Have chicks over..."

"Yeah crazy... That'd be wild...but we ain't got the bread, man."

"Yeah, I'm hip..."

"What a drag..."

Our rapport seemed perfect. We understood every nuance of each other's thoughts and feelings within that tiny and exclusive world of jazz that we wanted so much to be a part of.

Lester was a lean, very tidy boy, fussy about what he ate and what he wore. He didn't smoke and he didn't drink. The only vice he acquired later was smoking marijuana, to which he was introduced while on the road with a blues band. I suspected Lester was smoking pot, but he was discreet about it and never did it in my presence. Finally, when one of my other friends got me to smoke it during a jam session, Lester was delighted. "I'm so happy, man," he said, "Now, we can get stoned together." He seemed to have felt that pot was a secret that had come between us. After that, Lester and I did get stoned together and we would go to an amusement park in Long Beach and go on rides giggling like children.

I was disappointed with pot. Before I had tried it, my impression of the effects of drugs came mainly from Coleridge's opium-inspired poem, "Kubla Khan," which ends:

Beware! Beware!
His flashing eyes, his floating hair!
Weave a circle round him thrice,
And close your eyes with holy dread,
For he on honey dew hath fed
And drunk the milk of Paradise

I had hoped that the "high" I would get from marijuana would be such that I would be transported to a pleasure dome full of guilty and exotic secrets, or at the very least, that I would experience a state of euphoria and be happy. The only effect that marijuana had on me was that my sense of time and distance was distorted and I was inclined to giggle and act silly. I didn't find that particularly enjoyable and when I complained to Lester, he told me that one had to keep smoking pot for an extended period of time before he got a really good high. As a well brought-up Japanese boy, I was nothing if not conscientious. I smoked marijuana every day for several months, but I never experienced the magical "high" that I sought.

I think I had hoped that marijuana would round out my relationship with Lester, and he might have felt the same. He was so happy when I finally tried it. Even though we seemed to be so close, there was much that I could not share with him. I liked sports, and from time to time Yoshiro would take me to a Los Angeles Rams game. Lester would have thought that was square. I went bowling with members of my family and that was not something I talked about with Lester. Sometimes Lester would find me reading a book and I would find myself saying, "English class, man. A real drag." My relationship with Lester was further flawed by the knowledge that I would never be as good a musician as he. There was no doubt in anybody's mind that Lester would make it as a professional musician. He was lead trombone in the Los Angeles City College swing band, which, while we were there, was judged by *Metronome* magazine as the best college swing band in the country. Mr. McDonald, our hard-driving director, had me play third trombone to obscure my playing as much as possible in the middle of the four-trombone section. It seemed to me that he kept me in the band only because of my arrangements, which he played often. When, as winners of the *Metronome* contest, we did a professional recording for Columbia Records, Mr. McDonald selected one of my arrangements. Lester liked my arrangements too, but I thought he was just being loyal.

Music alone could not fill the void I felt in myself and in my life. I continued to read, not steadily, but fitfully and sporadically. For one of my English classes, I did a paper on the influence of Plato on Shelley without knowing much about either Plato or Shelley. The paper was received so well by the instructor that I began reading Plato's Socratic dialogues. I was gratified and happy when I found I could not only understand the dialogues but find pleasure in them. Socrates became a hero to me. I was in awe of his intellectual powers, his ability to question, and his endless patience in building grand logical structures piece by piece in such a beguiling manner. When I read the dialogues, I imagined that I was there in that circle of Athenians, sitting on the ground with my chin in my hands, listening to the old man talk. He became the father of my fantasy and when I got to Phaedo's description of his execution and read the words, "Such was the end, Echecrates, of our friend; concerning whom I may truly say, that of all the men of his time whom I have known, he was the wisest, the justest, and the best," I felt a deep sorrow, as though I had lost a father.

My distance from my parents grew while in San Pedro. It seemed that we hardly knew each other. There was nothing I could share with them. Language was the primary barrier, for my Japanese was inadequate to express anything but the simplest idea, and their English was even more primitive than my Japanese. "How can you not learn English after forty years in this country?" I would say rather cruelly to my mother. "It is such a difficult language," she would say. "And in Guadalupe, I didn't really need to learn English. And now... I'm much too old. I'm much too old to learn now." But language was not the main cause of the growing alienation between me and my parents. I did not think we had anything in common and it seemed to me that the cultural and intellectual chasm that separated us would only grow wider. In 1952, Congress passed the Walter-McCarran Immigration and Naturalization Act, which allowed Asians to become citizens, and shortly thereafter my parents were granted American citizenship. But their becoming American citizens seemed only to increase our distance, for they fell under the sway of Yoshiro's political tutelage. Yoshiro was a staunch, rugged-individualist Republican, contemptuous of Democrats, who, he believed, pandered to the masses. "The Republican party is a party of principles," he would say. Yoshiro, a Stanford graduate with a degree in economics, defended even the excesses of the free enterprise system such as the executives of General Motors giving themselves outrageously huge bonuses. He said there was more to running a big corporation than most people could imagine. It did not matter to him that neither General Motors nor any other American corporation would have hired him, no matter how good he was, because he was Japanese. My political views were no less stereotypical than my brother's, but they were on the other end of the spectrum. "The Republican party is the party of big business," I would say. "The Democratic party is the party of the people." I was not much concerned with politics; it was not a subject I could get emotional about. But it upset me that my mother and father registered as Republicans. They were also devoutly anti-communist and thought that Senator Joseph McCarthy of Wisconsin was a great man. I didn't know whether McCarthy was right or wrong, but I didn't trust politicians who went around accusing people of disloyalty. And I didn't know whether the Republican party was the party of big business or not, but it seemed to me to represent the established order, from my perspective, middle-class people who lived in fine houses and went to Presbyterian churches. The Republican party represented Santa Maria, and the Democratic party San Pedro and all those people with unusual last names. It left a bad taste in my mouth to see my parents identify with a party and with people who would not want to have anything to do with us.

With the money I earned working at the store I took piano and arranging lessons. My piano teacher was Dorothea Stewart, a woman in her early forties. When I first went to see her she was wearing a summer playsuit, which seemed rather daring for a woman her age. She smoked, seemed restless, and kept rubbing her bare legs with her hands. She was an animated talker with an expressive face and she impressed me as being very sophisticated. She lived in a small apartment high on a hill which had a wonderful view of the harbor and I was surprised that any abode in San Pedro could have such a view. I never met her husband, but she kept referring to him as "Jimmy" so I got the impression that he was younger than she. They separated shortly after I began taking lessons, so she moved out of the apartment and into her parents' house. What I liked about Mrs. Stewart—which I persisted in calling her even though most of her students called her Dorothea—was that she talked to me as if I were an adult. She made me feel very mature. She had a record collection of old English folksongs that she once played for me. One of the songs contained the words, "…as I lay in my bed with you in my arms…" It was only with some effort that I kept what I thought was an unruffled, sophisticated expression on my face. Gradually, I decided I was in love with her, so I told her I couldn't afford piano lessons anymore and quit. About a year later, I resumed taking lessons again, much against my better judgment. Mrs. Stewart would at times make me put my hand on hers while she played an arpeggio—so I could get the feel of how her hand moved, she said. Then, she would say, "You have very nice hands, Gene." I finally told her that I was going to quit again, and this time I told her why. I thought she would be upset with me for being so impertinent, but she seemed amused instead. She said there was no need for me to quit. But I could not see how I could continue to sit beside her on the piano bench for a whole hour and concentrate on playing the piano, so I did quit. I asked, however, whether I could come to see her one evening just to talk and she said that would be fine and that I could come later in the week.

When the evening of our appointment arrived, I was so nervous I decided to go to a bar and have a beer. It was a quiet neighborhood bar and only one other customer was there. I was twenty years old at the time but the bartender did not ask me for identification and served me a beer. While I was drinking it, I saw the bartender arguing quietly with the customer at the other end of the bar. Finally, he turned to me and said, "By the way, how old are you anyway?" I calmed myself and said, "Thirty-two." "What did I tell you?" the bartender told the other customer. Then turning to me, he said, "You know, you fellas all look a lot younger than you are." I had another beer and was feeling high when I got to Mrs. Stewart's house. I talked a great deal that night, about music, about how lonely I had been, about Plato and Socrates. I had been reading Oscar Wilde's "Ballad of Reading Gaol," so I recited what I remembered from that. "It's really true, isn't it, Mrs. Stewart," I said, "we do kill the things we love." Mrs. Stewart said she was fond of that poem, too, and she used to read it to one of her students. "Would you read it to me?" I asked. She said she would, but some other time.

I was happier than I had been in years when I left her that night. "Mrs. Stewart," I said, "I'm more in love with you than ever." She smiled and seemed pleased to hear it. I didn't even dare shake her hand.

The following day when I called her to ask when I could come to see her again, she had decided that she could not see me anymore. She said she was going through a period in her life when he had a lot of personal problems and she was not able to deal with mine as well. I was stunned. "But it was so wonderful last night," I protested. Besides all I wanted was to chat and read poetry together. She had promised to read "The Ballad of Reading Gaol" to me. Mrs. Stewart said she also feared that I might be a little unhinged. She said she had had a student who became enamored of her once before and they had spent an unpleasant afternoon together with him chasing her around the furniture. Did she really believe that I would chase her around the furniture? "Mrs. Stewart, you don't understand. You don't understand at all," I said, but she would not be moved. I kept telephoning and writing to her, asking her to see me just once more. I think I wanted to show her that I was reliable and that I would not chase her around the furniture. She finally relented, but when I arrived at her place there was a man there. The man said I must stop bothering Dorothea. He said if I persisted, he would call my parents. If that didn't work, he would call the police. And if that didn't work he and I would have to fight it out on the front lawn. I told him that I did not like violence and I did not think violence was a way of solving any problem. On the other hand, I had never backed away from a fight and if he wanted to fight I was willing to go outside and fight him. The man said he had not really meant the last part. Before I left I had a word alone with Mrs. Stewart on the porch and told her I would come to see her again in twenty years. She said she thought she would like that. Although I left with a smile, I was crushed and humiliated. It seemed like the darkest hour I had ever faced in my life.

It was only a few months later that I sustained another blow. My arranging teacher had been a man named Paul Villapigue, a very warm and affectionate man and a fine musician. When I was his student he had often expressed pride over how quickly and well I learned. He said I was one of the two best students he had ever had. I would call him at home when I had an arranging problem and he was always glad to talk to me. He had a small portable organ, the type used by missionaries, at his home and he would play passages and chords on it to demonstrate what he was about over the telephone.

Paul wrote a great deal for Charlie Barnett, and I went on two occasions to listen to the Barnett band rehearse. When Paul arranged a piece for Stan Kenton, he played the arrangement for me on the piano explaining all the intricacies, then took me to hear the Kenton band actually perform the arrangement. We were more than teacher and student, and once, when Paul was in a reflective mood, he told me, "You know, Gene, I'm really proud of the way you have learned. I feel almost like a father toward you." I wished Paul had not said that, for after that I became self-conscious about our relationship. I loved Paul and I did think of him almost as a father, but I had not actually put those feelings and thoughts into words. Fathers, and maybe mothers too, made me wary.

Several weeks later, I told Paul that I wanted to explore other approaches to arranging and he recommended another teacher for me. About a year later, shortly after my last meeting with Dorothea Stewart, Paul committed suicide. I never found out how or why. He was always having money problems and complaining about deadbeat band leaders who did not pay him. He had wide swings of moods which made me wonder at times whether he used drugs. He gave me one lesson lying on the floor and giving me verbal instructions on what to play on the piano. Sometimes, after a lesson we would go for coffee and as we walked down Hollywood Boulevard together, he would continue his lesson and illustrate his points by singing passages, oblivious to passersby who stared at him as if he were a madman. He did seem to have flashing eyes and floating hair. I wondered whether he killed himself because he had money problems, or because he had a problem with drugs, or both. It occurred to me that it would have helped him financially if I had continued taking lessons from him, even though it was only $8 a week. And I wondered if I had hurt him when I went to another teacher, and whether he had felt I had deserted him.

One evening, when my parents were both out, I took my father's canary and put it out of the house. Then, I made sure that the windows of my bedroom were tightly closed, disconnected the hose to the gas heater in the living room, and turned on the gas. There was enough space under my bedroom door to slide the end of the hose into the room. I stuffed clothing around the hose, then lay in my bed and waited. I could hear the gas hissing and I became very conscious of the physical functioning of my body, my breathing, the blood pulsating in my veins. I could feel the blood pounding in my forehead and in my ears. The surface of my skin began to feel cold and wet. I became acutely conscious of the fact that I was a living organism, one that was alive then, but would be dead in perhaps a few minutes. I was offended by the thought. I was more than just another organism. I got up and turned off the gas. I aired out the house, brought the canary back into the living room, and went to bed. A few weeks later I enlisted in the Army.

11

I was sent for basic training to Fort Ord in central California. Goro and Yoshiro had told me what the Army was like, and it apparently had not changed since they were in it. Lester would have hated it. He would have moped around the way he did during physical education class at school, saying, "Man, what a drag." I, on the other hand, liked it, even the "chickenshit," which was mainly people telling you to do stupid things just to show they could make you do them. The cadre once woke us up at midnight and ordered us to report outside with our footlockers. When we were all standing in formation carrying our footlockers, we were dismissed and told to go back to bed. I enjoyed such nonsense because it made me feel like everybody else. We all went back to our beds, saying things like, "What the fuck was that all about?" and "Goddamn chickenshit bastards." I adjusted easily to the ways of the Army. I remembered Goro once telling me, "In the Army you don't volunteer for nuthin'," so I kept that in mind. I also took care to line up in the middle of any formation and towards the rear, so that when the cadre picked people out for "shit duty" they were less likely to select me. Dressed in fatigues buttoned to our necks, our caps pushed down to our ears, we all looked the same and I found it easy to blend in with the crowd.

The first sergeant was a big, Black veteran of the Korean war with a chest full of ribbons. When he greeted us his eyes traveled down the line of recruits and a look of unutterable disgust came over his face. When he recovered from the shock of being faced with such a sorry lot, he said, "All right, young soldiers. I'm Sergeant Thompson. I am your first sergeant. I run this company, and don't you ever forget it. When I say, 'Shit,' you don't just shit. You squat down and ask, 'What color, sir?' My advice to you young soldiers is to give your souls to God, because from now on, until you leave this company, your ass belongs to me!" That was just the sort of thing I had expected a first sergeant to say, so I was delighted.

As it turned out, my ass didn't belong to Sergeant Thompson very long because I contracted viral pneumonia within a week and was sent to the base hospital. I was put in the critical ward where they began giving me massive doses of penicillin around the clock.

Late one night, I saw a tall figure dressed in black standing next to my bed. The room was dark, illuminated only by the light coming in from the hallway. Woozy as I was, I wasn't sure whether there really was somebody standing there or if I was hallucinating. I heard the man say, "Is there anything I can do for you?" When I didn't respond, he said, "Is there anything you'd like me to write for you? Is there anything you want to say to anybody?" Then it struck me. The man was a priest and he thought I was going to die. I was enraged and shouted at him, "Get out of here, goddamn it. Get the hell out of here!" I was proud of myself. A messenger of death had visited me and I had told him to go to hell. I have often thought afterwards that the priest might have saved my life. If he hadn't awakened me at that moment and aroused in me such anger and rage, I might have simply drifted off into an endless sleep.

During my convalescence the head nurse told me that at the height of the crisis my chest X-ray looked exactly like that of a patient who had died the night before. They had sent a telegram to my parents at that point telling them that if they wanted to see me, they had better come right away. It had taken several days for my parents to make the trip and by the time they arrived the crisis was past. I was a little embarrassed at seeing them. For the first time in my life I was on my own and within a couple of weeks I was flat on my back in a hospital bed. I was also embarrassed for them; they looked so out of place. The head nurse fluttered around like an anxious hostess, asking whether there was anything she could get for them. We spent an uncomfortable fifteen minutes together. My father said the Army had given them a very nice room where they could spend the night and even provided them with a meal, which he said was very good. My mother apologized for not coming sooner, but they had trouble arranging a ride. I told them it was okay; I hadn't been that sick anyway. There had been no need for them to come. My mother said she was happy to see me looking so well. They had feared that I would be lying unconscious and unable to talk. I told them I was fine and they didn't need to worry. That's good, they said. In that case, they would probably head home that afternoon. They were needed at the store. Yes, I thought that was a good idea. In all, I spent eight months convalescing and I celebrated my 21st birthday at the Fort Ord hospital. The head nurse brought in a cake saying Private Oishi was very lucky to have reached the age of majority. Later, because my X-rays would not clear up, I was sent to Letterman Hospital in San Francisco, which was called "the country club." We could go into town every night if we wanted and didn't have to come back to the hospital until morning. On weekends we didn't have to report in at all.

I went a few times to the International Settlement in San Francisco with a young sergeant from Idaho and made the rounds of the strip joints. There were cab drivers on the streets leaning against buildings who would say to us, "Ready to go yet?" One weekend I went with another friend to Caramel where we met two young women who worked for a bank in San Francisco. My friend liked the blonde, so I got the brunette, which was fine with me; she was the better looking of the two. She was 26 years old, slender, and looked Mediterranean with her large eyes and tawny complexion. I was extremely grateful to her; she was an angel of mercy, for during that one evening we spent together she made a man out of me.

When I was assigned to my second basic training company, I was an experienced soldier and I told my fellow recruits all sorts of stories, such as the time "I damn near got my ass court-martialed at the hospital for going A.W.O.L with a nymphomaniac nurse's aide from Oklahoma... built like a brick shithouse." The story was based on fact, though greatly exaggerated. There seemed to be an unspoken agreement that we believe each other's tall stories and take them seriously. I made friends easily and felt comfortable in basic training. I liked not having anything important to think about, not having much I really cared about, and being so tired at the end of the day that it seemed I was asleep as soon as I got into bed. But what I liked best was that everybody, except for the cadre and the company commander, was an equal.

While at Fort Ord I passed an audition for an assignment as an Army bandsman, so after completing basic training, I was sent to Camp Chaffee, Arkansas for eight weeks of band training. After that, I was shipped to Verdun, France.

I was assigned to a band stationed at a former French Army base called the Maginot Caserne. It was housed in a decrepit old building with a permanent sweet-sour odor. It had cracked tiles and crumbling walls. The building had a feel of decaying grandeur. There were high vaulted ceilings in the hallways, tall arched windows set in deep niches, and floral designs on the floor made of rose and pale blue ceramic tiles.

The Verdun band was located in what amounted to a supply

depot, and did not get many good musicians. About a third of the band were draftees, mostly college graduates. The rest were career soldiers, who impressed me as the dregs of the Army's musician pool. One of the first bandsmen to introduce himself to me was an older man, perhaps in his mid-forties. He was a professional private, a big-bellied slob of a man. He came over to my bunk with a photo album full of pictures of naked Japanese girls, whom he said he photographed while he was stationed in Japan. I handed the album back to him after a quick glance at its contents. "Don't you want to look at them, man?" He said looking surprised. "No, thank you very much," I said. "I think I've seen enough." I didn't like being spotted as a Japanese right off. I didn't think the man would have shown the pictures to a white soldier so soon after his arrival. I also didn't like the idea of this fat, slobbering degenerate lusting after Japanese girls.

In the beginning, I found some of the characters in the band fascinating. They were the kind of people I had never seen close up before. One of the trombone players, the man who had shown me the pictures of naked Japanese girls, stood by the garbage can at the mess hall in the evening collecting uneaten portions of meat. He said it was for his dog, but everyone knew it was for a German mistress he kept in town. There was a Jewish soldier from the Bronx who went around bare-chested flexing his muscles and beating on them to make them swell up. He was a drummer who liked playing the "Downfall of Paris" cadence, which the Germans were supposed to have used when they marched into Paris in 1940. The drum major of the band was a tall, good-looking corporal who said he had contracted gonorrhea six times. He sold cigarettes on the black market to finance his nightly whoring and "sucking pussy." There was a Black from Harlem who used to sit on his foot-locker and weave incredible tales of sexually warped adventures, which he claimed were absolutely true, every single word.

I wasn't sure what to make of these people. I was embar-rassed for the soldier who scavenged by the garbage can. As for the

Jewish drummer, I couldn't tell whether he was being sardonic when he played the "Downfall of Paris" cadence or whether he was a self-hating neo-Nazi. Neither could I form any judgement about the soldiers with exotic sexual tastes. I was thoroughly confused, both repelled and attracted by these characters who openly expressed thoughts that more conventional people like me would not have dared to utter. In some ways they seemed like liberated spirits.

By the time I got to Verdun I had been nearly a year in the Army. The excitement of being free from family constraints was wearing off and I began reexamining myself and my values. I tried reading the bible since we were all required to have one in our footlockers, but I soon concluded that there was little moral significance in it for me. The bible, the Old Testament in particular, was as cruel and bloody as the stories out of Japanese history and not nearly as entertaining. I turned to the Russians and for a period immersed myself in the dark, morbidly impassioned world of Dostoevsky. From Dostoevsky I went to Tolstoy, and from the Russians to Thomas Wolfe, in whom I thought I found a kindred spirit. What appealed to me was Wolfe's undefined yearning for what was lost and gone. My reading was guided largely by chance, by what was available at the post library and at the book stand at the PX—essays by Bertrand Russell and Alfred North Whitehead, a biography of Luther, a book called *The Wisdom of Buddha*, selected dialogues of Plato, which I bought and reread. One day, I came across a book by Sigmund Freud called *Moses and Monotheism*. I bought it because I remembered there was a work by Freud in the bookcase in Guadalupe that I used to leaf through now and again looking for passages that dealt with human sexuality—in other words, the "dirty parts." I was disappointed with Freud as an adolescent, but I thought I would give him another chance. I knew about Moses from reading the Bible, so I was intrigued by Freud's assertion that Moses actually was an Egyptian. It was like learning that the great lord Toyotomi Hideyoshi was a Portuguese trader,

or that George Washington was a shipwrecked Japanese fisher-
man who started a tobacco farm in Virginia. Freud's book raised
further questions in my mind about my own cultural and psychic
paternity. There was a darker fascination with Freud's book. In his
discourse on the primitive passing of power and authority from
one generation to the next, he wrote of sons slaying their fathers
and eating their flesh. I remembered how I didn't care whether
I saw my father again after he was arrested by the FBI. Patricide
intrigued me, not because I wished to do away with my father, but
because it seemed to me that, in my heart, I already had.

I read during the day because there was little to do after the
morning band practice. In the evenings I would go into town and
drink beer with a few of the people I chose as friends. The Verdun
band helped me see that I had choices as to whom I associated
with. Although I was on friendly terms with everyone, after duty
hours I avoided most of the men in the unit. The characters who
had seemed so intriguing at first were, I found, actually pathetic,
empty, and ultimately, not very interesting.

Some of us formed a combo and played a few evenings a week
at noncommissioned officers' and officers' clubs in the area. Each
of us was paid $12.50 a night for playing in the clubs. Those earn-
ings more than doubled my Army pay, so I had plenty of money. I
was even able to buy a car. When I was not playing with my own
group, I sat in from time to time at the enlisted men's place in
town, known as the Rex Club, where a career soldier and trumpet
player named Trummy Young—not the famous jazz trombonist—
held forth. Young had gotten lazy and musically stagnant through
his years of isolation in Army clubs, but he was a gifted jazz musician who was idolized by the Black soldiers who almost exclusively
patronized the Rex. I would drop by the club, and if Trummy needed another player, he would say, "Get your ax, man."

Most of the time my playing was mechanical. I followed the
chords and counted the measures. Once a Black soldier came up
to the bandstand, stuck his face in mine and said, "You don't

fool me, man. You're faking it. You're just faking it." I couldn't understand why he took it so personally and why it made him so angry, but he was right. At rare moments, though, my playing would for some reason take flight. I knew it when other members of the band would start saying, "Yeah, man!" and Trummy would look back at me with surprise on his face. Then I would start getting self-conscious and begin to lose it. So what I did on those rare moments was to close my eyes and just "wail." Those moments of inspiration were a mystery to me. They were gifts. I didn't know how to bring them on, and they ultimately caused me more pain than pleasure.

Many of the patrons of the Rex Club had never seen a Japanese person before. Some concluded I was Mexican because of a drooping Poncho Villa mustache I had grown. In fact, some called me Poncho. "Go Poncho!" they would say when I was playing well, "Go, man!"

White soldiers were not welcome at the Rex Club. The best-looking whores in Verdun, all white, worked out of the club, and they would not have anything to do with white soldiers. I was tolerated at the club because I had Black friends, I played at the club, and because the Blacks didn't know how to classify me. I don't know what would have happened if I tried to pick up one of the whores, but I wasn't interested in them. I was interested in a Black American girl named Lucille. She had come to Verdun as a dependent, but broke up with her husband, and when he was reassigned to the States, she stayed behind. She worked as a bartender at the Rex Club. I was feeling very loose when I first met her and said things like, "What's a nice girl like you doing at a joint like this," and, "Why don't you let me take you away from all this." Lucille, who called me Poncho, took it all very well, I guess, because I was in a happy and relaxed mood that evening and she saw I was having a good time. The next time I saw Lucille it was her day off, so we sat at a table, held hands, and danced. I didn't realize what a sensation we had created at the time, but the people

at the club were scandalized. The Black soldiers were just as paro-
chial and as narrow-minded as anybody else. They were offended
that one of their own, a Black, married woman, was carrying on
in public with an Asian. The manager of the club, a Black master
sergeant and a man of the world, took me aside and explained it
to me a few days later. He told me in a friendly way that holding
hands and dancing with Lucille in public was perhaps not the
coolest thing in the world to be doing. Someone must have talked
to Lucille too because she was careful after that about being seen
with me. Still, she seemed interested in developing a relationship.
Once, when I was playing at a service club at a nearby Army base
in Bar-le-Duc, Lucille showed up. It was clear that she had come
to see me because I had told her I would be there and it was an
all-white crowd. She had come with a white woman friend, but
she readily accepted my offer to drive her home. On the way, I
parked on the side of a country road. I wanted to kiss her, but she
would not allow it. She wanted to talk, but it seemed to me that
we had nothing to talk about. I was confused. "You ever going to
make it with me, Lucille?" I asked. "I'll make it, Gene," she said.
"I'll make it." What did she mean by that? What did I mean? What
did I want? I did not have an inkling of what Lucille saw in me or
what she expected of me. It was clear that we liked each other,
but when we parted that evening I had no idea how matters stood
between us.

When next I saw her, Lucille was sitting with a group of soldiers at the Rex. I went over to her, but one of the soldiers put his
leg on a chair to keep me from getting close to her. When I asked
her from across the table if she wanted to dance. Lucille just shook
her head. She looked anguished. When I didn't leave, she said,
"No, I really don't feel like dancing, Gene." "Oh, come on," I said.
The soldier barring my way said, "You heard her, man." "Is this
your old man?" I asked Lucille. "Please, Gene," Lucille pleaded,
"I really don't want to dance." I turned and walked away and the
snickers of the Black soldiers dug a hole in my back. After that, Lu-

cille seemed a little cool towards me. Perhaps she had expected me to fight, to knock that guy over who was barring my way. I decided to hell with her and to hell with the Blacks.

Paris was only a four-hour drive from Verdun, so I went there on my free weekends. Paris had opera, recitals, and good though somewhat outdated jazz in clubs on the Left Bank. I had started studying French as soon as I got to Verdun and towards the end of my two-year stay I could carry on simple conversations. I had a lot of accumulated leave time since I had not taken any furloughs while in the States, so I traveled widely in Europe for stretches of two to three weeks. I made one trip to Italy with a friend, but that proved unsatisfactory, so after that I traveled alone. I went to Spain, Germany, London, The Netherlands, and Denmark. I did all the things soldiers do when traveling. I also did things tourists are expected to do and visited almost every major museum in Western Europe.

Living in France and traveling in Europe made me see clearly for the first time that all white people were not like Americans, that the peoples of the white race differed from one another. And I saw that I, although of a non-white race, was more American than the white peoples of Europe. I was not pleased with that thought. I would have preferred to be more like a Frenchman.

The band gave me a farewell party at the Cheval Blanc, a local tavern where some of us hung out. Sometime during the evening, the bandmaster told me he was awarding me a good conduct medal. At first I was offended, but then decided he was joking and proceeded to get very drunk. Two of my friends had to carry me back to the Maginot Caserne that night and as the saying goes, poured me into my bunk.

In New York, the sergeant who typed up my discharge papers addressed me as "Corporal." He was middle-aged man with a heavy southern drawl, obviously an "Old Army" man who didn't recognize newfangled designations such as Specialist 3rd Class, which is what I was. We chatted a bit. He saw that I was RA or

Regular Army, not a draftee, so even though I was getting out, he was well disposed toward me. When he handed me my papers, he said, "Here you are, Corporal, and lots of luck." "Thanks, Sarge," I said. It was then that I discovered that the bandmaster had awarded me a good conduct medal. It made me feel as if I had failed. I had discovered something else. In the block designating race the sergeant had typed in "Cau." I had made the transition and it was official. I was a certified hakujin.

12

When I came home from the Army, my father and mother looked considerably older. My father had suffered a stroke that left him partially paralyzed so his walk was reduced to a slow shuffle. Outside the house, he picked his way timidly, poking the ground with a cane. He looked shrunken. Because of an infection, my mother had had one of her kidneys removed. She was still not fully recovered from the illness, but both my parents continued to go every day to the store to work. It was still thriving. Yoshiro had hired a second butcher, a part-time cashier, and a stock clerk.

I worked several months as an assembly line worker with the Douglas Aircraft Company, then enrolled in the University of California at Berkeley. The three years I spent at Berkeley were the happiest of my life. I was old enough and had seen enough to have some sense of what a special place a university was. In the first semester, I attacked my studies with quiet ferocity, but when I did a lot better than I expected, I relaxed. I had good friends with whom I got together on weekends to drink wine, play the guitar, and sing folksongs. I grew a full beard, wore more or less scruffy clothes, and thought of myself as Bohemian. My friends and I made occasional forays into the North Beach area of San Francisco where the beatnik joints were and felt very much a part of the contemporary cultural scene.

I selected what was then a new major at Berkeley called comparative literature, which had no set curriculum. With the approval of an advisor, I was able to pick and choose more or less as I pleased from among the offerings of the College of Arts and Letters. I had a glorious time. I didn't feel I was working very hard and frequently I wasn't. Most of the books I was required to read were those I would have wanted to read anyway. I was particularly interested in tragedy, which became my senior honor's project. I read Hamlet five or six times and every piece of commentary I could find on the play, for the notion of avenging a father's death was endlessly fascinating. Almost of equal interest was Greek tragedy. The savagery of the Greeks surpassed even that of the Japanese and that gave me comfort. I recalled how pleased I was in high school when the Latin teacher told of how the Romans, when defeated, would fall on their swords rather than be taken prisoner. Why, they were just like samurai, I thought. I liked Shakespeare's histories, not only for the drama and poetry but for the cruelty, savagery, and treachery they portrayed. The great men of English history were as bad as the great men of Japan. I was confused as a child when my mother read to me of how Tokugawa Ieyasu, who was supposed to be the greatest shogun of them all, broke his word to his dying lord. Instead of maintaining his lord's son and heir in power as he had promised to do, he assumed power himself. My mother could not explain how Ieyasu's supposed greatness squared with this treachery. He was a "great" man, my mother would repeat. He established a dynasty that lasted two-and-a-half centuries. At Berkeley, I saw that Shakespeare, too, did not mean "good" when he said "great." What he usually meant was a person of high birth and therefore with broad responsibilities. The rough equivalent in Japanese is erai. I used to be troubled by the word because it seemed to be applied indiscriminately to anyone who had attained power. President Roosevelt was erai. So was Prime Minister Tojo. So were Hitler and Mussolini, for that matter. My father had a picture of Napoleon in the living room before the war because he was erai. At Berkeley, my favorite play among the Shakespearean histories was *Richard III*. I was intrigued by this deformed, wicked, cruel, and scheming man who becomes king, and whom my parents no doubt would have called erai. At Berkeley, I began to understand that there were more ways of looking at the world than through the prism of conventional morality. There was something admirable about Richard; he was an extraordinarily courageous, strong, and resourceful man. He was also wicked and his wickedness contributed to his downfall, but he was a man of heroic dimensions, just like the usurper Akechi Mitsuhide, whom my father liked so much.

When I graduated from Berkeley in January of 1960, my parents offered to take me to Japan. My father had recently got a settlement from the government for business losses incurred because of the internment. Although it was only a fraction of his actual losses, the money had been unexpected and came as a sizeable windfall. My parents decided to use some of it to go to Japan, perhaps for a final visit, and offered to pay my way if I would go with them as their yojimbo, a bodyguard.

The first part of the trip was with a group of old people who, like my parents, had come to America from the Kumamoto Prefecture. So after two weeks of sightseeing in Tokyo, Kyoto, and other places of interest, we ended up in Kumamoto City. There was a group representing the city and the prefecture to welcome us. Young girls in kimono presented us with bouquets of flowers. There were newspaper reporters and photographs to record the return from America of these old natives of Kumamoto. That evening there was a banquet in our honor, which was attended by city and prefectural dignitaries, including the governor. My father was chosen to speak on behalf of the group. I had heard my father speak many times as a child. As the chairman of one committee or another, he was frequently called upon to speak at community gatherings. Nevertheless, I was a little apprehensive as my father poked his way with his cane to the front of the room.

"We left our native land more than a half-century ago," he said, "but our hearts and minds were always here. We have raised our children in a foreign land. Our flesh and blood became citizens of another country. We won and lost fortunes in America. We enjoyed great happiness and suffered deep sorrow. But what kept us striving during times of tribulation was that one day we would again see Nippon, our native land. In the morning, when we got up to go to the fields, we would look toward the glow of the morning sun. 'There in that direction is the sun,' we would say, 'Then, there, in that direction, lies Nippon, our land.' It gave us strength to face the day. Nippon! It was always Nippon that was in our hearts, in our dreams, and in our prayers. The land was our mother. She nourished and sustained us. She gave us hope, courage, and pride. And it is to her that we return after so many, many years... to our true home..."

When my father finished, people were wiping tears from their eyes and faces. I, too, felt my eyes growing heavy. "That Oishi," a man said at the next table, blowing his nose into his handkerchief. "He has a real gift." "Oh, sure," his friend said. "Oishi was a big man in his day, one of the biggest farmers in Guadalupe. He's no country bumpkin." There was relief and pride within the group that one of them had spoken so movingly and well before the local dignitaries. I don't think I've ever been so proud of my father as I was on that day.

Afterwards, there was entertainment. An amateur theatrical group put on a skit based on a regional song called "Otemo-yan" about a recently married young girl who, because of social complications, had not yet gone through the marriage ceremony. The skit, like the song, was comical, all the more so because it was in the Kumamoto dialect. The audience roared with laughter. Sitting next to me was our tour guide from the Japan Travel Bureau, a native of Tokyo. He sat with a bemused half-smile on his face. "Do you understand what they're saying?" I asked him. "Not a word," he said. "Do you?" "Yes, I do," I said. "I understand it pretty well." And I did. I truly did!

When we arrived in Nagasu the following day, it was like a homecoming even for me. My Uncle Yosaburo, Aunt Otsuru, and their children made me feel instantly like a member of the family. They called me by my Japanese name, Yoshitaka. I was amazed at how quickly I got used to that. Later, when I visited my cousins in Kumamoto City where they lived, they would call me Yoshitaka-san. And when I telephoned them, I would identify myself as Yoshitaka, as if that were the name I had used all my life.

Uncle Yosaburo was my father's younger brother. He and his wife had been in America and their five children were born there. But he had chosen to return to Japan around 1931, and with the money he had earned as a farmer in Guadalupe and with the help of some investors, he had started a small bank in Nagasu. He ran the bank, but he didn't look much like a bank manager with a day's growth on his face (he shaved only about twice a week) and open shirt, baggy pants, and worn geta on his feet.

Nagasu was exactly as I had pictured it. In our family album there were pictures taken in Nagasu, and although they were mainly of people, sometimes you could see part of a house or get a tiny glimpse of a street. I had formed a picture of Nagasu in my mind, which was remarkably close to how the village actually was. The main road was not paved and the spring rains made it a narrow ribbon of mud which was churned six times a day by the buses that linked the villages. A rare taxi would also splash its way through the village, but the main transportation was still the bicycle. Some farmers in the outlying areas had motorbikes, but Nagasu essentially was what it was a half-century earlier. "Nagasu will never change," my mother would say as we picked our way through the muddy street. My father would agree with a wan smile. I could not tell whether it was an expression of joy or sorrow. As we walked by the row of unpainted wooden houses, which over the years had been alternately burnt and bleached by the sun and battered and washed by the rains, I could believe that they looked no different than they did when my father was a child. There was now a movie theater in the middle of the village, but it was in an old building and one hardly noticed it except late at night when spectators spilled out into the street. Near the beach there was a new bar-restaurant, a pink stucco structure that appeared to be a doomed attempt at modernization. I often accompanied my parents when they visited former friends whose complaints had probably not changed a whit since my father left the village. "There's no hope for Nagasu," one man said. "There's nothing here. Even the fish are gone. Kumamoto and Omuta draw all the young people away. If we had a hot spring, one miserable hot spring, things might be different. Look at Tamana. Still another hotel going up there..."

The trip to Japan was not one of unalloyed or unremitting joy for my parents. During our stay in Tokyo, students were demonstrating in the streets against the renewal of the U.S.-Japanese defense treaty. My father was disgusted. They didn't have any understanding of foreign affairs, he said. They were just mindless dupes of the communists. When my father talked about it, he would do an imitation of the student demonstrators by staring into space with a dull, slack-jawed expression on his face. Partially paralyzed as he was, he was also frightened by the big crowds in Tokyo and other cities. He was distressed by the hectic pace of Japanese city life. He was fearful of thieves inside the hotels and of pickpockets in the streets. It seemed strange to me that my father was afraid of thieves in Japan when he did not seem to have such fears in San Pedro.

My parents, especially my father, had looked forward to seeing Bunraku, the classical puppet theater, in Tokyo. I had been eager to see it, too, especially since it would have given me the chance to hear joruri sung by a professional for the first time. But as luck would have it, the company was touring America at the time. Kabuki was out of season. "Ah, the season is very short nowadays," the hotel manager said. "You know, the young people don't like it much. They prefer movies and television. It's only the old folks who still go."

My mother had looked forward to doing some sightseeing at a more leisurely pace after we had settled in Nagasu, but those plans had to be canceled when she sprained an ankle while visiting the family graves. She had borrowed Aunt Otsuru's clothes to visit the graveyard and looked very elegant in a conservative brown kimono with a silvery hakama over it. But, no longer accustomed to wearing geta, especially on a path strewn with pebbles, she stumbled and twisted her ankle. One advantage of having a heavily bandaged ankle was that she could sit in front of company in her sprawling manner with less embarrassment. After her years in America, she could not sit in the proper Japanese manner with her legs folded under her.

When my mother's ankle healed sufficiently so that she did not need crutches to walk, we went to visit her older sister. Aunt Toyo lived only seventy kilometers away, but it took us nearly an entire afternoon to get to her farm. First, we took a train to Kumamoto City, then a bus to Omine village. From there, we hired a taxi to take us the last five kilometers.

The taxi driver was a young man about my age who spoke in a broad Kumamoto dialect. He was greatly impressed to learn that we were from America. "It was in the thirty-fifth year of Meiji that I went," my father told him. "Meiji thirty-five!" the driver said. "That was the year my old man was born. That's fantastic. It must be wonderful there."

The taxi stopped in front of an ancient-looking farmhouse from which an old man and an old woman emerged. Aunt Toyo looked like a caricature of a backwoods old woman with her straggly white hair tied in a knot behind her head, her back bent, her dark, callused feet poking out of the hem of a ragged kimono. The bottoms of her geta were worn almost smooth and the strap was made of rough hemp. When she spoke, we saw that she was nearly toothless. She was only a few years older than my mother, but she seemed to belong to another generation. My mother, by contrast, looked glamorous and chic with her dyed permanent-waved hair, a string of cultured pearls around her neck, a white embroidered blouse, and a western silk suit. The sisters had not seen each other since they were children and were like strangers. My mother bowed awkwardly. "Welcome, welcome," my aunt said. "Good that you came." "This is our youngest son, Yoshitaka," my mother said. "He came along as our bodyguard," my father added with a laugh, but the joke did not seem to register. "Ah... the youngest son," my aunt said. "So big...so big..."

The living room was barnlike and you could see the thatched roof through the exposed beams. I had heard that snakes often lived in thatched roofs and never really believed it, but I thought this was the sort of house where one might find them. The Shinto shrine in Nagasu was 800 years old and looked no older than this farmhouse. With dusk approaching it was getting cold and gloomy, but the old couple did not turn on what appeared to be the only light in the house, a naked electric bulb dangling down from one of the rafters. The house was bare of furniture except for a rough table apparently used for eating. There were a few scattered cushions, patched and flattened hard through long use.

My aunt served tea and we sat by the open door to take advantage of the fading light. Conversation came hard. The sisters seemed to have little to say to each other after their initial greeting. My uncle contributed little. He merely grinned and nodded. My father, who hadn't been eager to visit his in-laws anyway, retreated into silence, his face an expressionless mask. He would have like to have had a beer after a long trip, but none was offered.

Before supper, my mother prayed at the family altar. She rang a small bell, murmured a few prayers, and concluded by doing oshoko, putting pinches of ashes from one bowl to another. It was a ritual I had often done myself as a child at the Buddhist church in Guadalupe, but I never knew the significance of it. I imagined that my mother was praying to her mother and father.

I had looked forward to dinner since my aunt had indicated that she had made a big effort to prepare a feast, but there was neither fish nor meat. The main course was a bland dish consisting of carrots, potatoes, and few hard-boiled eggs. There was no sake or beer and I suffered almost as much as my father through the meal.

The following morning, the young taxi driver came precisely on time and greeted us cheerfully. It was a beautiful day. Women were out in the fields doing spring rice planting while swallows cut through the air above them. Their dress was similar to what my mother had worn when she had worked as a farm laborer in Guadalupe. My mother gave the equivalent of $500 to her sister before we left. She was very quiet on the trip back. "So old," she said once, almost to herself. "Such an old woman."

My parents stayed for two months in Japan and it was my impression that the trip on the whole was a disappointment. When they returned to Japan, they were struck by the meanness of its life. Uncle Yosaburo had one of the finest houses in Nagasu, but it lacked plumbing, water had to be pumped by hand, the bath water was still heated by building a fire under the tub. My parents were bored in Nagasu. For a while my father went daily to the noodle shop to watch sumo wrestling on television, but when the tournament ended he had little to amuse himself with. He grumbled about Yosaburo's stinginess in not buying a television set of his own. Japanese frugality, which he had praised in America, now seemed to annoy him. He would go shopping for his sister-in-law and buy eggs which he suggested be put in the morning soup, an extravagance Aunt Otsuru thought was just a little short of wicked. My father would also shop for the meat and fish, for, if left to Aunt Otsuru, there would invariably be too little to go around.

The annual village bazaar, which had so enchanted my father as a child now seemed to be a tawdry affair. The village, he complained, was full of suspicious-looking characters, con men, and pickpockets. "It's no different than it always has been," Uncle Yosaburo insisted, but my father remembered it differently. In the old days, my father said, real merchants and traders from the cities came, not the panhandlers and riffraff that now swarmed the village. The quality of the goods offered for sale used to be incomparably better, and there was none of this cheap junk. My father was also convinced that he was spotted on the first day of the bazaar as a wealthy man from America and the pickpockets were targeting him. He did not venture out again until the end of the week when the bazaar was over.

I planned to stay longer in Japan, but when my parents were ready to leave, I accompanied them to Tokyo to see them off. On the train, my mother reminisced about the old days when you could buy box lunches and hot tea in little earthen pots at the stations. She recalled how delicious those lunches used to be. They still sold box lunches and hot tea at the stations, but we were traveling first class and because of the air conditioning we could not open our windows to buy them. So we ate in the dining car, which was so severely air-conditioned that my mother caught a cold. When I parted with them at Haneda Airport in Tokyo, they were happy to be going home.

13

After my parents left, I remained in Tokyo for a week, then made my way to Osaka and Kyoto. It was a new and pleasant experience to be able to hide in a sea of Japanese faces that bobbed along the main thoroughfares of the cities, not to stand out, not to be looked at as a foreigner. My Japanese, which had been slow and halting when I first arrived, became fluent so I didn't immediately betray myself as a foreigner even when I spoke. But the big cities were expensive and beyond my limited means, so after a few weeks I made my way back to Nagasu. There was little to do there, but I enjoyed being with my uncle and aunt. They made me feel like part of the family. Even the house seemed familiar, although it was like no house I had ever seen before. The beams made of whole, crooked tree trunks were fitted together like a wooden puzzle held together by large wooden dowels that passed through the joints. "You can't find craftsmen who do work like this anymore," my uncle would say. He would pound on a beam and say, "Not one nail."

This might have been the kind of house my mother had in mind when she complained about the one in Guadalupe. There was a feeling of solidity sitting in the living room looking out on the garden with its pebbled walkway, gnarled pines, miniature mountains with their stone bridges and lanterns, all set against a backdrop of white camellias. There was an organic unity to the house, the garden, and the surroundings. The animals sensed it. Neighborhood dogs and cats would take shortcuts through the house when going back and forth between the street and the alley. Swallows nested in the rafters over the vestibule and Aunt Otsuru and her daughter Takako would have to sweep out the droppings. Aunt Otsuru would go to the door first thing every morning to let the mother bird out. "She's waiting and flies out as soon as I open the door," she said. The door was left open a crack during the day, and it was not closed for the night until the mother bird was in her nest.

My cousin Takako was two years older than I. Although she was not unattractive, she was unusually tall, which made it difficult to find her a suitor. When my parents were still in Nagasu they had hinted that they would not take it amiss if I took an interest in her. A cousin was not the best possible match for hereditary reasons, but Takako was not a full cousin. My father and her father were only half-brothers. My mother, who had gone to the public bath with Takako, went so far as to remark casually to me how large and full Takako's breasts were. I was too shocked to respond and pretended not to understand why she was making such an observation. One of my father's friends had also taken a sudden interest in me and had started introducing me to families with daughters of marriageable age. I began to suspect that my parents had had a hidden motive in taking me along to Japan. In Berkeley I had been briefly engaged to a white girl and that had put a scare into them. They wanted me safely married to a Japanese and where better to accomplish that than in Japan. I was annoyed with what appeared to me to be devious tactics on the part of my parents, but I dutifully went along with my father's friend on what were supposed to be courting calls. I pretended, however, that I had no idea why I was visiting these families and played the innocent with iron determination. Eventually, my father's friend gave up on me, no doubt convinced that I was hopelessly dense. Because of my parents' veiled hopes, I was careful to keep my relationship with Takako proper and correct. Nevertheless, I did risk one small outing with her. Since I first arrived in Nagasu I had been intrigued by the new pink bar-restaurant by the beach. One day I asked Takako if she would like to go there with me one evening. She said she would, but at her mother's suggestion, we chose a night when her father was out of town.

When we arrived, the American-style bar on the ground floor was empty. Most of the business was apparently conducted in the Japanese-style room upstairs. The bartender, who could not have been more than sixteen—most likely the owner's son—looked up at us sleepily when we sat at one of the tables. He slipped on a white jacket and brought us a drink menu. Takako was intrigued by the exotic names—gin fizz, Tom Collins, whisky sour.... We decided on a gin fizz and the bartender, scratching his head and consulting a recipe book, took a little time but managed to put together a decent drink. Takako first took a small cautious sip followed by a bigger one. Then she began to down it like a soft drink. She began to tell me about the memorable occasions in her life: her trip to Kagoshima with her graduating high school class, her trip to Miyazaki with the employees of her father's bank. She told me about the time she visited her brother at Beppu. He and his wife had taken her to a dance hall where her brother danced with her. She had drunk a glass of beer on that occasion.

"To me, this, too, is a trip," she said, tilting her glass. "And I could never have come if it weren't for you. Father would be upset if he knew I was here, but I don't care. I shall always remember this moment. In Kumamoto once, I saw an American movie. I thought how wonderful it would be if I could live like those people in the movie. It would not have to be forever, just a few hours would be enough." I reminded her that she was born in America, but she said she remembered nothing of it. She was an infant when her family left America.

We ordered daiquiris next, and when we finished them we left. We didn't talk much during our walk home. It was beginning to drizzle and the shopkeepers were putting straw mats on their merchandise. As we passed the noodle shop we could hear the laughter of men flirting with the proprietress, who giggled and playfully protested.

Although I liked the slow pace of Nagasu, after awhile I grew restless and made plans for another trip to the cities to the north. When my Uncle Yosaburo heard about my plans he expressed concern. "I know you're old enough to look after yourself. You've been in the Army, but I still owe it to your father. You know, when I was in America your father trained me. Whatever I am today, I owe to your father. I obey him still without question. If he told me to kill myself, I would do it. I wouldn't hesitate for a moment." My father always said that his younger brother Yosaburo had a weakness for posturing, so I did not take what he said seriously, but I did appreciate the sentiments he expressed and his concern, especially after I found out that what he had in mind was a drinking trip to the resort town of Tamana to celebrate his 68th birthday.

We started the evening with a bath at one of the hotels. The bath was the size of a small swimming pool with an artificial waterfall and surrounded by lush tropical plants. The bubbling, sulfurous water was so hot I feared I would not be able to bear it and would fail my uncle's first test. Gritting my teeth, I lowered myself inch-by-inch into the steaming water. I felt like Ishikawa Goemon being boiled in oil, but once my skin stopped prickling the water was quite pleasant and relaxing. My uncle stepped into the bath, immediately immersed himself up to his neck, and said, "Aaaaaaa," with a look of exquisite pleasure.

After the bath, my uncle ordered a masseuse. I declined a massage saying I was ticklish and instead ordered a beer which I drank dressed comfortably in a cool cotton kimono. "The trick is to relax," Uncle Yosaburo explained. "When you get to be my age, there's no greater pleasure than a hot bath and a massage. A sad state of affairs, but it is true, nevertheless."

My uncle also had a beer afterwards, then we got back into our street clothes and started making the rounds of the hotels for some serious drinking. My uncle, being a bank manager, appeared to be a frequent visitor at all the places. The waitresses knew him by name and were unrestrained in their flirting. Uncle Yosaburo feigned embarrassment and said to me, "You needn't tell your father about this." I knew that my uncle wanted to see how well I could hold my liquor, so I tried to drink slowly, but nevertheless got pleasantly drunk on countless little bottles of hot sake. I sang, I danced, I flirted with the waitresses, and had a wonderful time. We were both in good spirits when we tottered out into the street and headed for the train station, but Uncle Yosaburo decided we needed one more for the road when he spotted an American-style "standing bar," something of a misnomer since everyone usually sat on western-style stools and chairs in such establishments. We were immediately surrounded by hostesses in western clothes. We ordered whisky and I danced with one of the girls who pressed her body against mine in a most suggestive way. I told her I was with my uncle and had to behave myself. "I could tell you stories about your uncle," she said.

When we walked out, Uncle Yosaburo said, "Be careful of places like that. It's safe for me because I know the owner. But you go in as a stranger and you'll find at the end of the evening that you've bought every girl in the house a drink."

We didn't get to the station in time to catch our train. The next train would not leave for another hour so Uncle Yosaburo decided to go home by taxi, an unheard of extravagance. "You needn't tell your father about this," he said, and this time he meant it.

`The taxi fare was 1,000 yen, about $2.85 at the time. My uncle had the driver stop a few hundred yards from the house. "We'll say we came by train," he said. The mistress of the dress and kimono shop saw us alight from the taxi. She greeted us and smiled knowingly. "Damn busybody," Uncle Yosaburo murmured.

When we got home, Aunt Otsuru had our dinner laid out for us. "Did you return on the 9:30 train?" she asked. "Unh," Uncle Yosaburo grunted, meaning yes. "It took you half an hour to walk from the train station?" she persisted. Her husband was too occupied with his food and seemed not to hear. Aunt Otsuru gave me a sidelong smile and I discreetly smiled back.

I was in Japan for six months, and I spent the last two months in Kumamoto City because I could get a room in a small inn there for 75 cents a night and eat for less than a dollar a day. Three of my cousins also lived and worked in Kumamoto City so I visited them from time to time.

I became especially friendly with Rinjiro, Uncle Yosaburo's second son, whom I visited several times. He was about the age of my sister Hoshiko, or about 34 at the time. He was six years old when his family left America, and his memories were mainly of the farm on which they lived. While in America they lived in Oso Flaco, an area not far from Guadalupe but so isolated that you could occasionally see bears feeding on the blackberries that grew along the river. In our many long discussions, we often talked about how fate had dealt with each of us. Although there was a seven-year age difference between us, we could have switched places. Uncle Yosaburo could have stayed in America and my father could have decided to return to Japan as he had always intended to do. Our fascination for one another was to a large degree due to our attempt to see in each other what we might have been.

My Japanese was not up to a serious discussion of politics and economics, but Rinjiro, a young executive at a local transportation company, tailored his remarks, without condescension, to a level I could understand. He was concerned about what he saw as Japan's swing to the left and the development of a welfare state. He thought the leftists, the communists especially, were hypocrites "just like the Russians." Rinjiro had an abiding hatred for the Russians, and one evening he told me about his wartime experience to explain why. But his story told me a lot more. It showed how differently World War II affected his life as compared to mine. Although the thought came only later to me, I had been imprisoned in Arizona during much of the period Rinjiro talked about.

"I was in Manchuria during the war," Rinjiro said. "I was drafted when I was seventeen, towards the end of the war, and rushed to Manchuria. Our division was made up of nothing but smooth-cheeked youngsters. We replaced the Kumamoto First Division, a crack outfit of battle-hardened veterans, which was transferred to Saipan for the last-ditch battle in the Pacific. We were put into their place like a bunch of scarecrows. That's all we were, put up to give the impression that there was still a Japanese Army in Manchuria. None of us had ever seen any combat or had any training to speak of. Equipment was so short at the end of the war that our training was conducted with wooden poles. All the trainers did was beat us. That's what the Japanese Army called training, just systematic beatings for no reason. They would line us up and an officer would go down the line slapping each of us across the face as hard as he could. I had leave to visit my family before we were shipped out, but I didn't go home. My face was so swollen I was ashamed to be seen by my parents.

"Anyway, there we were in Manchuria towards the end of the war, young, untrained, and scared recruits standing guard. We were no match for the Russians when they attacked. They just rolled over us as if we weren't there. And they took no prisoners, the Russians. I will never forget it and I will never forgive them. They were barbarians. They went through the battlefield looking for the wounded. We could hear our men moaning and screaming as they were killed. Four of us spent three months running and hiding from the Russians. We lived like bandits, raiding farmhouses for food as we made our way to the coast. We were constantly on the verge of starvation. We once found enormous mushrooms in the woods, but didn't know whether they were poisonous. One of the men volunteered to try them first. He said he was so hungry he didn't care if he died. We watched him for maybe half an hour and couldn't wait any longer. We ate our fill of raw mushrooms. We got terrible diarrhea but nothing worse than that.

"When we got to a port city we ran into a Russian patrol. We ran in every direction and in the flight I got separated from my comrades. I don't know what happened to them. I never saw them again. I hid until nightfall and made my way into the city. I was desperate. You can imagine how I looked. I was dressed in rags and covered with dirt and mud. But in the darkness I was able to make it to the waterfront. There, a rice merchant still had his lights on. When I walked in there was a big commotion. I thought of turning and running, but I swallowed hard and stood my ground. They called the master of the house, a tall dignified Chinese with long white whiskers. Using sign language I asked for something with which to write. I had learned some Chinese in school, so I wrote as best I could that I was a Japanese soldier. I asked for mercy. I saw no point in lying. He could see what I was without my telling him.

"Later the man told me he had been impressed with my penmanship. I had always been strong in penmanship in school and that counts for a lot with Chinese as it does with Japanese. He also saw that I was just a youngster. Luckily, I have small, smooth features and looked even younger than my eighteen years. I lived with the merchant for more than a year, posing as his son when Russian patrols came looking for Japanese soldiers. When the Russians left, I was able to get on a British freighter bound for Yokohama. The merchant urged me not to go. Japan would be in ruins, he said. I could continue to live with him as his son. He was, indeed, like a father to me, but I told him I wanted to see my own country again and he understood. I shall never forget him as long as I live. I corresponded with him after I got back to Japan, but when the communists took over he stopped writing. I stopped writing, too. I was afraid it might be dangerous for him if he got letters from Japan.

"When I first got back to Japan, I was ashamed of having survived the war when so many of my comrades had died. I did not want to be seen again in Nagasu, but I wanted to see my father and my mother just once more. I checked the schedule and picked a train that would get me into Nagasu at midnight. I intended to see my parents and leave again before dawn before any of the neighbors spotted me. But, of course, once I was home there was no more thought of leaving."

My cousins wondered how I was occupying my time alone in Kumamoto City and teasingly asked whether I had found somebody special. I told them I was doing a lot of sightseeing. But they were right. I had found somebody. Her name was Toshiko. Both her parents were dead and she supported herself working as a hostess in a "standing bar" in Kumamoto City. She had a woman's face, rather severe, almost aristocratic, but a small, childlike body, which was probably the result of malnutrition. Toshiko was a consumptive, and though she had undergone a cure, she did not have much faith in it. She said she never made any long-range plans. So it did not matter, she said, that I would go away in a few weeks and that we would never see each other again. "I don't plan for the future. I decided you have to enjoy life as you live it."

During the day, we often took short trips to points of interest near the city. In the evening she would go to work and when she finished she would come to my inn where we would spend the night together. Part of the appeal I had for Toshiko, I now think, was that I was foreign. She often talked about visiting Paris one day, even though she insisted she made no long-range plans. I told her I visited Paris many times when I was in the Army, but she didn't ask me any questions about what it was like, perhaps because she didn't want to disturb the pictures in her head. I had thought I was being very Japanese in my relationship with Toshiko, but she used to say that I didn't walk like a Japanese. She thought the way I soaped myself in the bath was extremely funny. Instead of rubbing the soap on a washcloth I would apply the soap directly on my body. Once when she came to my room and I kissed her on the cheek, she became upset. She thought it was crude and ill-mannered of me to start the sex act so soon after her arrival. I told her in America people kiss as a greeting. It was no different from bowing or shaking hands. "Oh...." she said. "A greeting.... Then it's all right."

Toshiko personified the whole of my experience in Japan. I felt very close to her, but there was no deep commitment. I knew that our parting would be sad but not tragic. I would remember her with fondness, even with love, but it did not trouble me that I would never see her again. Even while we were still together, she had become as insubstantial as a memory.

I myself began to feel like a creature without substance during my final weeks in Japan. The anonymity that I had liked so much palled on me. On my last train ride to Tokyo, there was an American couple sitting across the aisle. I had not spoken or heard English for months and it came almost as a shock that I could understand every word they were saying. The woman had a *Time* magazine sticking out of her handbag. I wasn't able to read Japanese newspapers and I had trouble understanding newscasts, so I did not know what was going on in the world. I asked the woman if I could read her magazine. She looked surprised that I spoke her language, but passed the *Time* to me without comment. Senator John F. Kennedy of Massachusetts had just won the Democratic nomination for the presidency. I was not very interested in politics then, but that bit of intelligence seemed extremely important. I was like a starving man. I read every word of that article, then proceeded to devour the rest of the magazine from cover to cover. I even read the ads.

My brother-in-law, Icy, Hoshiko's husband, came to meet me at Los Angeles International Airport. He, like my brothers, had served in the Military Intelligence Service and had been in Japan as part of the occupation forces after the war. As we swung onto the freeway leading into town, the broad, gently curving expanse of concrete, which at times had seemed so oppressive, suddenly looked beautiful.

"It's good to be back," I said. "I know what you mean," Icy said.

14

Although I had decided to give up music, I had not wanted to pursue a course of study at Berkeley simply because it was likely to lead to a job. As a music student, I had thought of myself as a free spirit, someone living for art for art's sake, and I could not get myself to think so soon in practical terms. By the late 1950s there were a few professional job possibilities for Japanese, but they were mostly in scientific or technological fields, or in public school teaching. My brother-in-law Icy had a degree in marketing from UCLA but was working as a produce clerk for Safeway. I didn't know, therefore, what I could do with a degree in literature; it would probably be useless as far as getting a job, but I was in a mood to take risks. I used to say with bravado, "I want to study something worthless." When I graduated from Berkeley, however, I was already 26 years old and beginning to worry more about earning a living. I had originally planned to do graduate work in either comparative literature or English, but decided instead to go to law school. My Berkeley friends who tended to think of lawyers as shysters or stuffed shirts teased me about my decision, but I justified it by saying I didn't really want to be a lawyer; I only wanted to continue my education in a specialized branch of the liberal arts. Look at Petrarch, I would say. He was a poet, a scholar, a diplomat, and a mountain climber. There's nothing wrong with being versatile.

I was accepted at the Berkley law school and put on the waiting list at Harvard, but chose the University of Michigan Law School because, I told myself, I wanted to experience the great American heartland.

Michigan, when I first arrived there, seemed like the promised land. At the university and in the town of Ann Arbor where it was located, there seemed to be none of the anti-Asian prejudice that existed in California. The people were friendly. Strangers would greet me in the street and old ladies would engage me in conversation. I had no difficulty meeting girls. At Berkeley, I had only had one girlfriend, a graduate student in music, who dressed in black and, like me, thought of herself as bohemian. But at Ann Arbor I dated girls who did not seem to feel they were doing anything extraordinary or risky by being seen with me.

The atmosphere at the Michigan Law School also contrasted sharply with Berkeley, but not in a way that I liked. The students there were not as relaxed or as intellectually curious as my friends at Berkeley. They were already looking ahead to the bar examination and many of them already saw themselves as corporate lawyers in a prestigious big-city firm. They envisioned a big office in the tallest building in town, exclusive clubs, a chic and beautiful wife, a tree-shaded home in the suburbs, and two cars, His-and-Hers, in the garage. They were self-assured to the point of being pompous and rigid beyond their years.

After a few months at Michigan, I began to find it impossible to study. Instead, I wrote poetry, listened to music, or did watercolor paintings, often all night. During the day, I slept instead of going to classes. I tried, but I could not break out of my lethargy. I would sit at my desk in front of an unopened law book for perhaps fifteen minutes, then walk away without having lifted the cover which seemed to weigh a ton. It was only years later, under psychiatric care, that I understood that I had been suffering from depression, probably since I was a teenager. It was a condition that was not widely recognized as a mental disease at the time.

My social life served as an escape from the drudgery of work. For the first time in my life I had more women friends than men. One of them was a psychology student from Switzerland named Sabine who was attending the Merrill Palmer Institute in Detroit for a year of graduate studies. I met her at a party in Detroit and eventually the relationship developed into a love affair. Sabine, who could not have looked more like a hakujin with her blonde hair and blue eyes, seemed very Japanese to me. I thought she appealed to the Japanese side of my nature. The Swiss, I thought, must be very much like the Japanese in their values and outlook, and indeed they are, as I later discovered. They resemble each other in their peasant attitude toward work and thrift, in their compulsion for self-effacement, and their exaggerated concern for the good opinion of their friends and neighbors. But much of the appeal we had for each other did not come from the Swiss in Sabine or the Japanese in me. Sabine's mother was the daughter of Walter Rosam, a German painter and a Jew who died fighting in the German Army during World War I. Sabine's father, a Swiss journalist, met her in Frankfurt in 1933 when he went to Germany to write about the Nazi takeover and the violence being directed against Jews. He married her within a year and took her back to Switzerland, no doubt saving her life.

Switzerland is a country where natives of villages five kilometers apart will view each other with suspicion. Swiss German, moreover, is a language that defies mastery by anybody but a native and it doesn't help that one is a speaker of High German. It might even be a hindrance. It meant that Sabine's mother was forever "the foreigner" in her adopted country. Some of Sabine's many relatives, moreover, did not like having a Jew in the family and family ties were strained. For Sabine, it meant that though she was from a solid Swiss family, she was touched by foreign elements and emotionally, at least, not fully secure in her own country. These were all matters that Sabine and I discovered only years later, when I was beginning to understand that when I said "Japanese" I often meant a state of alienation or sometimes of isolation. At Ann Arbor, I just accepted our love as one of life's mysteries. My favorite symphony at the time was Beethoven's Third. The lighthearted playfulness with which the finale begins made me think that Beethoven must have been in love when he wrote it. If Tchaikovsky's Sixth was my death song, Beethoven's Third was a reaffirmation of life. I was experiencing an emotional breakthrough. I was no longer earthbound, tied to my past. I had taken Sabine into a hot-air balloon and cut the tether. We would go soaring off together into a world of our own. As we walked down the street, I would sing to her, "We will dine on, we will thrive on, just plenty of kisses, just mister and missus, in our little blue room...." Even so, when that magical year ended and we parted in New York, we did not know for sure whether we would ever see each other again. I went back to San Pedro and later enrolled in a graduate program in journalism at the University of California at Los Angeles. Sabine returned to Zurich, but we corresponded and wrote passionate letters to one another. After about a year, we decided that I would go to Switzerland to meet her parents, relatives, and friends.

Sabine's house was located in an affluent suburb of Zurich. Between the street and the house was a terraced garden with large apple trees, well-tended flower beds, and towering rhododendrons. Walking through the sturdy iron gate and up the cool, shady path to the house, one got a sense of quiet comfort and well-being. Sabine's father, a foreign editor for the internationally respected *Neue Zürcher Zeitung*, was still at work. Her mother and sister had gone ahead to the family chalet in the Alps, where we were to go the following day, so only the maid was there to greet us. As we walked into the entrance hall, I saw that the walls were crammed with oil paintings and I remembered Sabine telling me that her father was a collector. The living room, which looked out to the garden, was lined with books, and like the entrance hall, pictures were hung on every available bit of wall space. There was a numbered lithograph by Miró on one wall and an original Vlaminck on another. The furniture was a tasteful mixture of antique and modern and there was a Steinway grand in the dining room. I was led to the third floor, past a gallery of somber oil paintings. One that stuck in mind was that of a big fish hanging by a meat hook. Sabine put me in her room, which was next to the maid's. It was filled with Chinese and Indian artifacts, some of which her father had brought back from his travels. I knew that Sabine had an affinity for Oriental art. The thought flashed through my mind that perhaps I was her latest acquisition. I said I wanted to rest for a while, so Sabine left me alone in the room. From the window, I had a clear view of Lake Zurich and could see sailboats in the distance. I wondered whether I had made a mistake in coming. I was out of place in a setting such as this.

Sabine's father was a tall, ascetic-looking man, dark-skinned and almost East Indian in appearance. He was courteous and civil but not overly warm or friendly. He was a man who was not capable of dissembling and it was clear to me from the start that he was opposed to my marrying his daughter. His transparency was a quality I learned to appreciate in later years, but at the time I experienced it as deep hostility. We had our first private talk in Wengen, a small alpine village surrounded by a ring of snow-covered peaks, the most majestic of them being the Jungfrau. We sat on one of the third-floor verandas of the family chalet, which Sabine's grandfather had bought. It sat on a hill, so from the veranda we could look out over the village and down into a valley some 3,000 feet below.

Sabine's father did not mince words and asked some pointed questions. I was at the time a graduate journalism student at

UCLA. He asked me what kind of job I thought that I, as a Japanese, could get in America. I told him I didn't know, but that Sabine and I would not get married until I had a job. He asked me whether Sabine was the first white girl I had dated. He told me that I would not inherit any of the family wealth, that I would have to sign an agreement relinquishing any claim to it. If Sabine died, her money would go to her children, if any, not me. He asked me what kind of a life children of mixed racial parentage could be expected to lead in America. By then I was beginning to bristle. It seemed to be that I had never been so humiliated, but I told him as calmly as I could that while I might have had some difficulties in my life, I had managed to survive. My children would have difficulties, too, though most likely not as many as I. And they would also survive. No life is without difficulties, I told him, and each of us must face them as individuals and overcome them as individuals. That would apply to my children, just as it applied to everyone else. Sabine's father spoke English well but not colloquially, and he might have had difficulty understanding me. He disagreed with what I said, and expressed the opinion, which sounded more like a decree, that we should not have any children at all. Some twenty years later, when we discussed this conversation, he insisted that he could not possibly have said such a thing. In the meantime, he'd had three grandchildren on whom he doted, so he might have had difficulty recalling that he once objected to their being born.

I knew from Sabine that her mother was passionately opposed to our marriage, but when we first met at Wengen she greeted me with warmth. It must have taken a heroic effort to be friendly and it took a toll on her. Sabine told me that her mother's behavior when they were alone together was almost hysterical. She wept and had emotional tantrums. The strain was too much for her mother so she and her husband returned to Zurich sooner than planned, leaving us only with Sabine's younger sister Barbara, who let me know right from the start that she was on my side. I had a wonderful time in Wengen with just the three of us there. We went on long hikes during the day, through pine woods, across pastures, and on trails cut into pale green mountainsides dotted with wild flowers. The air was fresh and fragrant with the smell of warm grass and flowers. As we walked, new vistas of deep, green, winding valleys would open up in front of us. Mountain peaks draped with snow and ice rose out of the evergreens. In the evening we sat on one of the verandas and watched the setting sun turn the snow on the Jungfrau the color of strawberry ice cream. We played the guitar, sang, and drank wine. I wanted to stay there forever and dreaded our return to Zurich. When we did go back, I developed stomach cramps and had to go to a doctor who could find nothing wrong with me.

I did not know precisely how I felt about my trip to Switzerland when I got back to Los Angeles and UCLA. But I knew that I was unhappy. I could not get myself to write to Sabine. I did not even write her parents to thank them for their hospitality. My instinct was to walk away from it all, to turn my back forever on Sabine, her family, and Switzerland. One day, Professor Wilcox, chairman of the Journalism Department, came up to me looking uncomfortable and embarrassed. He told me he received a letter from a girl in Switzerland inquiring about me. She wanted to know whether anything had happened to me. It was none of his business, he said, but perhaps I should write to her to tell her I was all right.

I did write to her, and a year later, after I got a job at the Associated Press, I went to Switzerland to marry Sabine. After our wedding, my relationship with Sabine's parents grew into friendship. I developed a special fondness for her mother Lilo. Years later, when we lived in Germany and my German was good enough so she could talk to me in her own language, she told me about her life as a young girl in Berlin, about how she worked as a secretary and about one of her love affairs. Hearing those intimate details from her past made me feel closer to her. When she died in 1975, I mourned her as a friend.

As for my parents, they had resigned themselves to the strong possibility that I would not marry a Japanese girl. Their one remaining worry was that my wife, whatever her race, would be unsuitable. When I showed my mother a picture of Sabine, however, she began to worry that I might be unsuitable for her. She looked "erai," my mother said. As always when my mother used the word, I was not sure what she meant by it. But I think she meant that Sabine looked as if her social status was much higher than mine. At our wedding in Zurich, when the telegrams of congratulations were read, there was one from my parents to Sabine's parents, in which they expressed the hope that I would prove myself worthy of their daughter. When my mother finally met Sabine, she was greatly relieved. She took me aside and said with a bright smile, "I like her. I really like her!"

During the first two years of our marriage, while I worked for the Associated Press, we lived in Los Angeles. We went once a week to San Pedro to do our grocery shopping at my brother's store and to have dinner with my parents. At first, my mother made an attempt to serve Western meals. She began serving Japanese food, though not without misgivings, when I assured her that Sabine preferred it. My father was astonished that Sabine liked misoshiru, a strongly flavored soup made with fermented soy bean paste that is peculiarly Japanese. He often quoted an American missionary, who once told him that one can never learn to speak Japanese until he learns to like misoshiru. That Sabine should take to it so quickly seemed remarkable to him. My father was also surprised that Sabine could understand American television. After all his years in America, my father still could not clearly understand newscasts or the dialogue in movies. When Sabine and I sat in the living room watching television, my father would say to Sabine "You understand?" When Sabine said yes, he would shake his head with wonder.

After each of our visits, my father would give Sabine a bag of fruit to take home with us. On one occasion he took her aside and gave her a hundred dollars, telling her that she was not to give it to me but to spend it on herself. Sabine was extremely moved and delighted with the gift and I felt a twinge of jealousy. But I was also pleased that my parents were able to accept a hakujin daughter-in-law, which in the past would have been unthinkable. Such a marriage would have been viewed as a family tragedy. It might have helped that Sabine was not American. She was an immigrant like themselves, someone with whom they could identify and sympathize.

15

In 1963, when I was completing my studies at UCLA, I began looking in the help-wanted section of the magazine *Editor and Publisher*
for newspaper jobs. I wrote mainly for newspapers in New En-
gland because I figured that the farther I got from the West Coast,
the better my chances would be of getting a job. I think I also had
in the back of my mind the idea of one day being Editor Webb of
Thornton Wilder's *Our Town*. But none of the newspapers replied.
One of them added the line, "Please enclose photograph," to its ad
shortly after I wrote to it.

As it turns out, I didn't need to travel very far for a job because
I was hired by the Los Angeles bureau of the Associated Press as
a newsman. Luck played a big role. Several months earlier, one
of the professors at UCLA had given us an AP writing test that he
had found in a journalism journal. When I applied for a job at
the AP, I was given the same test. Hub Keavy, the bureau chief,
in announcing my employment, wrote: "He passed the writing
test with flying colors!" I would have felt more secure had I been

hired without that bit of fortuitous help. At the time, I knew of no other Japanese working for a white news organization (I learned only later that Bill Hosokawa, the nisei writer, was working as an editor for *The Denver Post* at the time). I was such an anomaly at the bureau that people coming into the office would mistake me for a copy boy.

My colleagues at the AP were friendly and helpful and I learned a great deal about writing and reporting in the first year. By the second year, however, I was getting disillusioned with the job. We did not do much original reporting. Most of our work consisted of rewriting stories from *The Los Angeles Times* and *The Herald Examiner*. I was sitting every day next to newsmen with ten years of experience or more, and doing the same work as they. I had told Hub Keavy, the bureau chief, that I wanted someday to be a foreign correspondent and he had said that would be possible. He mentioned one newsman who had started out at the Los Angeles bureau and who was now working overseas. But I had difficulty imagining my being plucked out of the Los Angeles bureau one day and being sent to Paris, which was where I wanted to go. I could more easily see myself sitting in the Los Angeles bureau twenty years later—doing agricultural market reports, rewriting other people's stories, and editing and filing overnight copy on the late shift.

After a year and a half at the AP, I used part of my vacation to take a trip to the East where I visited *The Baltimore Sun*, *The Washington Post*, *The New York Herald Tribune*, *The New York Times,* and *Time* magazine. None of them gave me any encouragement except *The Baltimore Sun*. Paul Banker, then city editor, interviewed me, had me take a general knowledge and a writing test, and said he might be in touch with me. I felt I had done poorly on the tests, so when I got back to Los Angeles, I was downcast, thinking the trip had been a complete failure. Within a month, however, Banker wrote and offered me a job as a reporter at $98 a week. After Sabine and I stopped jumping up and down, I called him to accept and, at

Sabine's prodding, told him that by the time I got to Baltimore, I would have two years of experience. He chuckled and raised the offer to $108 a week, which was three dollars more than I was making at the AP.

Working at *The Sun* helped me understand better what I had missed at the Associated Press. It was not simply the satisfaction of seeing and hearing things firsthand. What was just as important to me was the idea of being part of the most important and the most powerful newspaper in the city, an institution that some loved and respected, others feared or hated, but nobody ignored. The Associated Press, while nationally and internationally a much larger organization, had not been an institution I could identify with. Early in my career at *The Sun*, when I was the education writer, the city superintendent of schools remonstrated with me because I had not called him up for a comment before writing a story. "From now on, I'm going to deal with radio and TV," he said. "Okay," I said. "If you're telling me you don't want to talk to *The Sun* anymore, that's all right with me. I have other resources." The following day, the superintendent called me up to apologize. "I think I need you a lot more than you need me," he said. That was a heady experience. Later, when I covered state government, I felt or at least acted as if I were on an equal footing with the attorney general, the comptroller, state legislators, and judges. I was a reporter for *The Baltimore Sun*, and that made me important, too.

If you want to succeed at *The Sun*, you tried to turn in two or three stories a day and worked until the early morning hours on Friday on stories for the Sunday and Monday editions. The idea was to have your byline in the paper every day of the week. I had never worked as long and as hard in my life, but I was happy.

What I liked most about being a reporter was that I could be close to events without being personally affected by them. I could attend meetings, demonstrations, talk to people in every walk of life, go to the scene of a crime or a disaster, write about issues laden with controversy and passion, but my own life remained untouched by what I witnessed and wrote. I believe I had a notion that by observing events as a reporter and by writing about them for a newspaper, I was in control and immune from the effects of the events I was describing.

After my third year at *The Sun*, I was assigned to cover state government. Two years earlier, Spiro T. Agnew had been elected governor of Maryland, so my primary responsibility was covering his administration. Though a Republican, he had been elected as a liberal. Gradually, during the period I was covering him, he became more conservative, particularly on racial issues. He was reserved and aloof, so I never got to know him or like him very much. And when he started to shed his former liberal image, I saw him as an opportunist and began to distrust him and his politics. I never thought, however, that he was corrupt and accepting bribes, as was later revealed to be the case.

When Agnew was selected by Richard Nixon to be his running mate, I was given the biggest reportorial plum then available on the local staff—coverage of the Agnew vice-presidential campaign. Several weeks into the campaign, however, the assignment soured because of an incident that thrust me into the national spotlight.

On a trip from Las Vegas to Los Angeles, Agnew came to the back of the place where the reporters sat and, seeing me with my eyes closed, asked, "What's the matter with the fat jap?" I heard the remark but pretended to be asleep, hoping to spare myself the need to react to it. When Agnew left, however, the reporter sitting next to me asked, "Did you hear what Agnew called you?" I lied. I said, "No, what was that?" "He called you a fat jap." I said, "Well, that goddamn fat Greek."

That should have ended the matter, but Agnew's remark was reported and it became a widely publicized election issue. His press aides began telling inquiring reporters that Agnew and I were good friends and that "fat jap" was my nickname. It was only then that I got openly angry. It seemed to me that the suggestion that I would answer to such a nickname was degrading. I also began to wonder whether Agnew's staff, with whom I thought I had been on good terms, had been calling me "the fat jap" behind my back. It was these thoughts that prompted an indiscretion on my part as Agnew was island-hopping in Hawaii.

While flying over Oahu, the pilot came on the intercom and said, "If you will look out to your right, you will see the United States naval base of Pearl Harbor." A devil must have been sitting on my shoulder and whispering in my ear, because I leaned over to Herb Thompson, Agnew's press secretary seated in the row ahead of us, and shouted, "Bombs away!" Thompson pretended he did not hear me, so I shouted again, "Bombs away!" Thompson still did not react, but Homer Bigart of The New York Times, who was sitting next to me, was doubled over with laughter. He went down the aisle, saying, "Did you hear what Oishi said? He said 'Bombs away!'"

Members of Agnew's staff were upset that the traveling press accompanying Agnew did not report my "bombs away" remark, and they went out of their way to have it reported. They finally succeeded in getting Maxine Cheshire of The Washington Post to include it in one of her columns. When I learned of that, I called up Richard Harwood, then national editor of The Post, and tried to get him to intercede, but without success. I then called Paul Banker, my managing editor, who seemed amused by the whole thing. He told me not to worry about it, but I remained apprehensive for days after the Cheshire column appeared. I think I expected reprisals from some quarter.

What struck me about the reaction of Agnew's staff to my "bombs away" remark was that we had clearly become enemies. Their attitude appeared to be that if the press was out to "get" Agnew, then they would do what they could do to "get" me. That is the only explanation I could think of for what a member of Agnew's staff told Jules Witcover, a political writer who was working on a book on Agnew. The staff man, who remained anonymous in Witcover's book, noted that we had spent the night in Las Vegas the day before the "fat jap" remark, which was true. Then he went on to say that I had started to play craps and had lost heavily. He said he helped me work my way out of my losses, but I would not leave the table. I continued gambling all night until it was time to leave, and even then I had to be bodily dragged away from the crap table. On the plane, he told Witcover, my complexion turned green. He had never seen anybody's skin turn that color before. They called the doctor accompanying Agnew to examine me. Agnew, when he saw me, became quite concerned. "What's the matter with the fat jap?" he asked in alarm. He insisted that the doctor examine me again.

If I had not been a bit paranoid already, this story would have made me so. Except for the "fat jap" quote, not a word of the story was true. Witcover, with whom I was friendly, suggested that I sue the man for libel. He said that if I put him on the witness stand, he would identify him as the man who told him the story. He had no idea how weird and unsettling the situation was for me. Like Kafka's K, powerful people were out to get me. I was not going to give them another opening by filing a libel suit. If I did, there would be more lies, each more elaborate and vicious. What I told Witcover at the time was, "I'm not going to get into a pissing contest with a skunk," but my fears went far deeper than that flippant remark would indicate.

I was shaken by the Agnew incident, for it put me in the national spotlight as a Japanese. Being known far and wide as "the fat jap" was like having a target painted on my back. The notoriety would not die, in part because many assumed that I took pride in having achieved national fame of sorts, even if I experienced it as humiliation. A reporter for *The Des Moines Register* covering the Nixon campaign in 1968 asked me for my autograph, and he could not understand why I was offended. On election night, two Republican women serving cookies at Agnew's election headquarters in Annapolis gushed, "We're so honored to meet you." At a New Year's Eve party I encountered an attractive young woman at the punch bowl. It was a neighborhood affair, at the house of good friends, so I at least recognized everyone there. But I had never formally met this woman, who, smiling sweetly, said, "fat jap." Not, "Hi, how are you," or "Hello, I'm Jane Doe," but "fat jap." I was paralyzed by the remark. I wanted to say something cutting, but no cutting words came to mind. I just stood there with a reflex smile on my face until I was able to turn and walk away without a word. It was one of many similar encounters that would be repeated over and over again, and I never got used to them. They had a corrosive effect instead. Each time I heard the words "fat jap" or a reference to the incident, it hurt a little more, like someone cutting into an open wound. It was a powerful indication that something was wrong. It was not merely the epithet "jap" that cut me, it was more the reminder that I belonged to a despised race against whom America had fought a long and bloody war. Not everyone remembers or even knows about the mass incarceration and the vicious anti-Japanese propaganda promoted by the government during World War II. Race transcended citizenship, nationality, character, friendships, everything. A jap was a jap and could not be trusted.

16

When I was promoted and sent to *The Sun*'s Washington bureau, some assumed I was sent there to cover Agnew. I had worked hard at *The Sun* and had earned the promotion. It was galling that some people thought it was due to Agnew. The Agnew incident also diminished the sense of security I had as a *Sun* reporter. In an unlikely, grotesque way, it shattered the illusion that I was immune from the consequences of the events I was reporting.

So as happy as I was about the promotion, I was not in the best frame of mind when I went to Washington. I covered economic affairs at first and later Congress, but after I settled into Washington coverage, the job began to trouble me. In the Washington bureau, we rarely had time to work on exclusive stories. We usually covered the stories that every other news organization in town was covering. It seemed to me that with the intense, concentrated, and competitive coverage, our standards should have been higher. In fact, they were lower. On the local staff, I never cribbed information or quotes from wire service stories, mainly because

I didn't trust them. In Washington, I found to my dismay that every correspondent took quotes and facts from wire service stories and used them without attribution, as if he or she had personally dug up the facts or heard the remarks being made. When I saw that not only my colleagues at *The Sun* did this, but also those at *The Washington Post* and *The New York Times*, I began to do it, too. The term "pack journalism" had not yet been coined, but I felt strong pressures to keep pace with the pack and became somewhat less happy with my profession.

As a local reporter, it bothered me when I suspected that people were not telling the truth, but it did not change how I felt about my profession. In the early 1970s in Washington, the topic of the day was the war in Vietnam, and truthfulness and the reliability of information were issues in themselves. It was not enough to accurately report information you got from your sources; you had to worry about whether they were lying, or whether they themselves even knew what the truth was. Reporters have always had to worry about the truthfulness of their sources, and as bad as the so-called credibility gap was during the 1970s, most reporters were able to live with it. I, too, was able to cope, but I had more difficulty than most, for I had by then read enough about the wartime experiences of Japanese Americans to know how the lies and distortions of people in high positions had affected my life. It had not been a help to me and other Japanese Americans that those lies and distortions were accurately reported and attributed.

In 1942, shortly after the Japanese attack on Pearl Harbor, Frank Knox, then Secretary of the Navy, visited Hawaii and upon his return to Washington told reporters, "I think the most effective fifth column work of the entire war was done in Hawaii, with the possible exception of Norway." We know today that there was no basis of truth for that statement by Knox, but the press at the time gave it wide coverage. At about the same time, stories appeared in U.S. newspapers saying that downed Japanese pilots were wearing school rings from Honolulu's McKinley High School, that resident Japanese had cut arrows in cane fields pointing the way to Pearl Harbor and set up barriers to block military traffic, that they had broadcast false radio signals to confuse U.S. defenses, that there were plans to poison the water supply. There was not a bit of evidence for any of this.

When I was in Washington, I not only distrusted Administration sources, I distrusted the anti-war doves in Congress almost as much. But I continued to do my job as professionally as I knew how. I do not believe anyone could have detected from reading my stories how uncomfortable I felt when I wrote them.

In 1972 I was sent to Bonn, West Germany, to take over *The Sun*'s bureau there. In the beginning, I concentrated on covering East-West détente, which was the dominant issue of the day, and traveled with other members of the foreign press corps to cover various international meetings. When my German improved to the point where I could conduct interviews in the language, I began traveling alone. I went more frequently to East Berlin, which had intrigued me from the beginning. The first time I crossed from West to East Berlin, I was strongly moved as I saw from the train window the barbed wire fences, dog runs, anti-vehicular barriers and trenches, and sentry boxes. There had been a period in my life when I, too, had lived behind barbed wire, guarded by soldiers with machine guns. It struck me hard to see from the other side of the barriers how ugly and cruel were the means devised to keep people penned in their own country. I began to understand what my colleague Peter Kumpa used to say when I played the devil's advocate for the Soviets. "If you think it's nice on the other side, you ought to go there." The barbed wire, the concrete, and steel that sealed off East from West had a greater impact on me than any ideological argument concerning the freedom of expression and movement. They were immediate and tangible, as was the boorish East German border guard who looked at the photograph in my passport as if trying to memorize my every feature, then looked up at my face, then down again at the photograph, then up again at my face. I later learned that every guard did that to everybody, but it was unnerving the first time and I never got completely used to it.

In stark contrast to East German officials, I found the people of East Berlin and East Germany friendly and open. They were more old-fashioned than the people living in the West. The higher standard of living in the West appealed to them, but they didn't like what they saw on television about crime, drugs, juvenile delinquency, and what they considered moral degeneracy. One West German correspondent living and working in East Berlin told me he liked the people in the East better than those in the West. The political system was cruel and stifling and life was harder in the East, he said, but perhaps because of that people helped each other more, relationships were closer, and family ties seemed stronger. Even so, thousands of people were either fleeing or emigrating to the West ever year, not only from East Germany but from the Soviet Union and other parts of Eastern Europe. Some of the younger refugees from Eastern Europe no longer spoke German, but they claimed to be Germans. Some might have been what people called "Volkswagen Germans"—those who claim to be German for purely economic reasons. Some no doubt were, but I got the impression from those I interviewed at refugee camps that they were experiencing a genuine feeling of having come home. I also talked to former refugees who were already settled in West Germany and learned from them that the feeling of homecoming was sadly not one that was likely to last. Many ethnic Germans, some of whose ancestors settled in the East centuries earlier, felt like foreigners in West Germany.

I met a woman in Bonn, a former refugee, who told me about her childhood in Silesia. She told me about how, toward the end of World War II, as the Red Army approached, she and her family loaded their belongings onto a horse-drawn wagon and made their way west. She was a so-called "expellee," one of those who fled or were driven out of Germany's "Eastern Territories," which became part of Poland after the war. I talked to other expellees and read as much as I could find on the experiences of German civilians living in Eastern Europe during the last days of World War II. Millions of Germans, civilian men, women, and children were driven from their homes. About a million people were known to have died and about a million others were still unaccounted for. I was deeply moved by what I heard and read, all the more so because much of the world probably felt that these Germans, even the children, deserved what they got, so strong was the anti-German hatred engendered by the war.

There were several "compatriots" associations in West Germany made up mainly of former refugees or expellees from the East. They were organized in much the same way as the Japanese associations were in America, grouped according to where the people originated. The West German associations, however, were more politically oriented. They were vociferously anti-communist and anti-détente. As a group, the former refugees tended to be doctrinaire and right-wing, but I found they had very human and moving stories to tell. The charter of their national umbrella organization had this to say: "We have lost our homeland. The homeless are strangers on this earth. God has placed man in his homeland. To separate him forcefully from it is to kill him spiritually."

"Heimat" is a sentimental sounding word which means "home" or "homeland." It has the same emotional pull as the word "valley" in *How Green Was My Valley*. In my talks with former refugees I heard it used often. I envied them the concept, the notion of having an identifiable place on the map that was "home." If I had to name my heimat, I could not do it.

My experience in Germany awakened in me a desire to look into my own roots, so when my family and I returned to Baltimore in 1976, I took a year's leave of absence from *The Sun* to write an autobiographical novel. But the book, instead of providing answers about myself, raised a host of questions that I was not prepared to face at the time. I tried to get at some of these questions tangentially by writing about other ethnic groups when my leave of absence was up. I wrote about Soviet Jews who had come to Baltimore, Blacks moving to the suburbs, Black Muslims, new Korean immigrants, lonely old people, vestiges of the civil rights movement in Mississippi, neighborhood problems, about churches, and religious sects and cults. It was the most interesting assignment I had ever had, but it was also the most demanding. I had no time or space limitations, no deadlines other than those I set for myself. My stories got longer and longer and the time I took to write them began to stretch from days, to weeks, to months. There was always one more person to interview, one more document or book to read. The last project I worked on at *The Sun* was a series on the Ukrainian community of Baltimore and I found myself reading and writing about the Ukraine in the sixteenth century. The series was never published. Even as I wrote them, I suspected the articles were not publishable. They were too long, too cautious, and too dry. It had become a compulsion for me to get the stories "right," to get the historical and human perspectives, and I tied myself in knots trying to write stories that were complete and accurate and at the same time not hurtful or damaging to the people I was writing about. There were stories I spent weeks researching and never wrote because I did not think I understood them well enough. One such story dealt with my visit to B'nai Israel, the oldest functioning synagogue in Baltimore at the time. It was located in the former Jewish quarter in East Baltimore. There were still a few Jewish delicatessens in the neighborhood, but virtually all the Jews had moved out of the area years ago. The rabbi was an immigrant from Poland, a very quiet, sad looking man, who declined to be interviewed. He said I should just attend one of the services and I would understand more about the synagogue that way. Besides, he said, they sometimes had trouble getting a minyan, the obligatory ten adult males, and they might need my presence. Although I was not Jewish, I might do in a pinch, he said. Before the service, the rabbi showed me around the synagogue. The sanctuary was only used, if at all, on high holidays, and services were now held in a small anteroom. The congregation was made up only of men, mainly downtown business and professional people. I watched the men dribble in one after the other and saw how they were transformed as they put on their yarmulkes, their prayer shawls, and opened their prayer books. As they murmured their prayers, rocking back and forth on their heels, this group of American businessmen, accountants, and lawyers became Jews. It seemed to me that if I could have attended a service in Poland in the nineteenth century, it would not have differed in essence from what I was witnessing in this crammed and dusty anteroom of an East Baltimore synagogue. Later, I tried to find a word to describe the atmosphere. "Oriental" first came to mind but that was not right at all. "Non-American" popped in my head, but that was further off the mark. Then it came to me, and the word was "private." For me, everything that is close and personal had been Japanese, non-American, and private. And what I had witnessed at B'nai Israel also seemed private. I read what I could find on the history of Jews in Baltimore and talked to old people about the childhood memories of the old Jewish quarter. I went back twice to B'nai Israel in an attempt to understand what I was seeing in terms of its history and tried to capture the atmosphere in words, but I could not do it. And even if I could, I felt it was not for me even to attempt it. I would have been an intruder into a part of the human heart and mind that was sacred. These men, it seemed to me, were not only communing with their God, but with their fathers and their fathers' fathers and with a part of themselves that had grown largely irrelevant to the world around them. It seemed to me that they went to pray in this dying synagogue in a dying neighborhood because it made them feel whole. I envied them and I wished I could have formed part of the minyan.

Working for *The Baltimore Sun* had been like being part of a family, but I began to feel I had outgrown it. I wasn't sure whether I could go back to news writing and I was having more and more difficulty writing stories about people. I began to feel isolated at the paper. I felt almost as I did in Guadalupe after the war, when Norman asked me, "All you japs coming back?" *The Sun*, where I had spent some of my happiest and most productive years, no longer seemed like a home to me.

In 1979, Harry Hughes was elected governor of Maryland. I had met him ten years previously, when he was a state senator and I was covering the legislature. We had always got along together and I liked and trusted him, so when he asked me to be his press secretary, I accepted.

17

It was not easy to leave *The Sun*. Paul Banker, now the managing editor, was angry and upset that I was quitting. He had been under heavy pressures to increase circulation by changing the look and the style of coverage of the paper. The changes went against his conservative approach to the news and against a tradition that went back more than a century. When I left *The Sun* I felt as if I were deserting him, and he might have felt the same way. During my last talk with him in his office I tried to thank him and to tell him how much *The Sun* had meant to me, but I got choked up and had to stop. Banker, a very reserved man, looked ill at ease. We parted without telling each other our thoughts.

I took the job as press secretary because I was no longer comfortable as a newspaperman, but I rationalized my decision by saying that for once in my life I wanted to be on the inside looking out instead of being a perpetual outsider trying to look in. I also had some notions of public service. The Vietnam War, the Watergate scandal, and the corruption of officials in Maryland had greatly damaged the credibility of people in government. As a knowledgeable and scrupulously honest spokesman for a reform governor, I thought, I could help heal the rift between government and the press.

Being the son of my father, I might have also liked the idea of being regarded as a big shot. A friend who happened to be sitting at the bar of a Baltimore restaurant when Sabine and I were having dinner there, came by our table to tell us that he overheard the owner telling the waiters, "That's the Governor's new press secretary in there." When I walked into the State House, the guards often greeted me by name. They hadn't noticed me at all when I was a reporter.

There was a great deal of bickering over turf and status at the beginning and the staff was soon divided into factions. I was reminded of my visit to Beppu, Japan, where there lived a tribe of monkeys. They came down from the mountain and sat on a hillside overlooking a park and tourists would throw peanuts to them. There was a clearly visible hierarchy of chiefs and subchiefs, their females, and young ones. While the lesser monkeys scurried around for peanuts, the chiefs and subchiefs moved slowly, with great dignity, like characters in a Kabuki play. They would only deign to eat the peanuts that happened to be at their feet and let the rest lie. None of the smaller monkeys, however, dared to pick up a peanut that was close to one of the chiefs. It was said that there was a "king" monkey, but few had ever seen him because he stayed at the top of the mountain and rarely came down to the park with the rest of his tribe. I tried to keep those monkeys in mind at the State House. I bought a big picture of a gorilla which I put up in my office with a sign under it reading, "The Press Secretary." It was supposed to remind me not to make a monkey of myself, but, as I told a few of my friends, the longer I looked at the gorilla, the better looking he got. It was difficult to be detached, to maintain a sense of humor and balance in an atmosphere in which so much energy was expended to preserve or increase power and status, and in which the size and location of your office, the number of secretaries, the size of your chair, the color of your telephones took on great importance, if not in your own eyes, then in the eyes of others. The pettiness and bureaucratic infighting, which at times got mean-spirited and vicious, began to wear on me.

When I took the press secretary's job I thought my good standing with the members of the press corps, many of whom were friends, would make my job easy. I dressed mainly in sport coats and, unlike my predecessors, never wore three-piece suits. I didn't own one. I was pleased when one of my former colleagues at *The Sun* laughingly said, "You dress just like a reporter."

I did very much want to remain a reporter. While I was no longer happy as a newspaperman, I needed the reporter's identity, the sense of security, the feeling of belonging that I had enjoyed through most of my years with *The Sun*. But the illusion that I was still somehow part of journalistic fraternity was impossible to maintain. A few weeks after I was on the job, a wire service reporter, who had once worked for *The Sun*, came into my office and demanded an immediate interview with the governor. When asked why he needed to talk to the governor so urgently, he refused to say. I tried to explain to him that if I forwarded his request, the first question the governor would ask me was why he wanted to see him. I thought our relationship had been friendly when we were colleagues at *The Sun*, but the man, instead of engaging in a conversation with me, took out his notebook and began writing down what I was saying, as if to indicate that every word I uttered could be used against me. So I was already on edge when he said to me that he would not tell me the subject of his inquiry because if he did, the governor and I would put our heads together and concoct an answer. In other words, we would be able to lie more effectively. At that point, I lost control of myself. I shouted, "You goddamn fucking asshole." I kept shouting that until the reporter, alarmed, backed out of my office and left. I had never had my honesty or integrity questioned in such a manner, and I could not stand it. My secretaries in the outer office had heard me shouting, and I was greatly embarrassed. I apologized to them and promised I would never again behave in such a manner. And I didn't. But it took me some time to get over my outburst because I did not fully understand what had caused it.

It is, of course, in the very nature of a press secretary's job to be disbelieved or at least treated with cautious skepticism. I should have known that, for I could not count the number of press spokesmen I had so treated over the years as a reporter. But I was not prepared for reporters, especially former colleagues, not believing me. In the beginning, I overcompensated for my discomfort by being too candid and providing "leaks," which made me an object of suspicion within the governor's staff. I was not the only person talking to the press, only the most visible one, but I was suspected, or so it seemed to me, of being responsible for every leak and for every embarrassing or damaging statement attributed to an anonymous "member of the governor's staff." I had the feeling that there were those who were whispering in the governor's ear about my indiscretions, mistakes, bad judgment, and possible betrayal. It might have been largely paranoia, but as it is often said, even a paranoid has enemies.

I began to feel that I could not find refuge even in my own home. Sabine had been very much against my leaving *The Sun*. She thought I was foolish to leave a newspaper that had been so good to me and had given me so many opportunities. She also thought I was unsuited for a press secretary's job and would be unhappy in it. She was right on both counts, but it probably would have been better for our marriage if she had not been so clear-sighted. While at *The Sun*, when not under deadline pressures, I often asked Sabine to read my articles before I submitted them. She was always glad to read them and offer suggestions. When I was at the governor's office, she took little interest in my work and declined to read speeches I wrote for the governor. It seemed to me that she was disassociating herself from my job and perhaps from me.

At one point, after I had left *The Sun*, Sabine said she considered a journalist "a prince among men." Her father, of course, had been one, and she had married one. She was trying to explain to me why she had been so disappointed when I had left *The Sun*, but she stung me with that remark.

We spent our vacation in Switzerland that first summer after I left *The Sun*. We went to Wengen. We had gone there often, especially during the period we lived in Bonn, and I had many happy memories of the chalet, the village, and the surrounding country-side. But I could not enjoy Wengen as I once did. I felt weak. In the past we had gone on long hikes, but I no longer felt up to them. Climbing exhausted me. I was convinced that I had mononucleo-sis, for I had been working long hours in my new job. I went to a doctor for blood tests, but he could find nothing wrong with me.

Because of my job, I had to return to Baltimore a week earlier than my family. I fantasized about the airliner carrying my wife and children crashing into the ocean, and I was not sure wheth-er that was what I feared or what I wanted. It seemed to me that I was beginning to disintegrate. I went to a friend, a medical researcher who was also a psychiatrist by training, and told him about my fantasy. I told my friend that I felt as if I were a jigsaw puzzle that I had very carefully and painstakingly put together over the years, and now the puzzle was falling apart and I no longer knew who or what I was. He recommended some practicing psychiatrists and eventually I went into psychotherapy, and later into analysis.

When Sabine returned from Switzerland, she was appalled by what seemed to be intense anger rising out of me. "Why are you so angry with me?" she asked. I was not capable of answering that question because I was not aware that I was angry. To the contrary, I thought it was Sabine who had grounds to be angry, for I had been carrying on flirtations with women at Annapolis and had come home smelling of perfume and with lipstick on my collar.

I told my wife that I needed time to myself to work things out in my mind, and she consented to my renting an apartment in Annapolis. Renting the apartment had been my idea, but when I was alone late at night, I felt as though I had lost my home and was all alone in the world. I bought a revolver, which I kept loaded at all times. I slept with it in my bed. Sometimes I would cock the hammer and hold the barrel to my head. I had no serious intention of pulling the trigger, but it gave me comfort to know that I had in my hand a weapon with which I could instantly put an end to my life if I so decided.

Having affairs became a compulsion with me. I did not like myself very much and I liked even less what my new job was doing to me. It was making me into somebody I did not recognize and I needed to know that I was still a likable, lovable person. I had several relationships with women, and I did not make much of an effort to hide them from Sabine. I even told her about one of them.

As far as the rest of the world knew, the reason I had the apartment in Annapolis was to avoid the daily commute from my home in Baltimore. I did return on weekends to Baltimore, but my relationship with Sabine was strained. I also had difficulty talking with my children. Elisabeth, our oldest daughter, was fourteen. While in Bonn, she had had academic difficulties, so when we returned to Baltimore, we enrolled her in a private school, hoping she would get more individual attention there than in a public school. Elisabeth was at the time considerably less mature socially than other children her age, particularly American children. We had worried a little about the snobbery and the cliquishness found in private schools, but this was a Friends' school, where such things were thought to be minimal. Elisabeth was virtually an outcast during her years at Friends' and she suffered greatly. I suffered, too, for I could not help but suspect that her being half-Japanese had something to do with her social isolation. Sabine's father might have been right. Perhaps it was wrong for me to have children. I almost disliked Elisabeth for her unhappiness. It made me feel guilty and helpless. I didn't know how to help her except to shout at Sabine to tell her to leave Elisabeth alone and not to nag her so much about doing her homework. Our other children were Eve, who was twelve, and Peter, who was nine. I had little contact with them during this period. I was afraid to get too close to them. I remembered how much I had suffered from my father's outbursts and I was afraid of doing the same to my children. My mother said that Papa once told her that when he became angry he felt as if he were all alone and that he had to fight the whole world by himself. I, too, felt as though I were isolated and was ready to explode at the slightest provocation. I also felt as though I had become something I was not and was no longer my children's father. I hated getting telephone calls from reporters at home, especially radio reporters who wanted to record my comments. I did not like my wife and children hearing me talk in that stiff, cautious, pompous, and at times evasive style of a press spokesman, in short, like a hakujin. I did not like being a phony in front of my children; it was humiliating. I later learned that they were impressed by my being able to talk like that, but at the time we were not speaking to each other very much.

After two years, I resigned as press secretary. My explanation was that I wanted time off to complete my book on the Japanese American experience. That was true as far as it went. I did indeed intend to take a year off to complete my novel. But the real reason I quit was to save my marriage and my life. Whatever my problem was, I knew it had something to do with my race. I thought by working on my book I would find the answers I needed to go on.

18

I had long thought that I and probably most Japanese Americans
of my generation were mental cripples, but I could not define
with any precision or clarity the nature of the disability. In 1976
when I first began work on my novel, I found myself breaking
down in tears while writing. When I looked at what I had written, the passages did not seem emotional enough to cause such a
reaction. One passage that choked me up was about a character
who declared to himself, after his father's death, "I am Japanese."
During that period I began to have trouble talking to people, especially to groups. My lips would freeze up at unexpected moments,
and it was only with the utmost physical exertion that I could
make myself talk. There was one occasion when it seemed as if my
whole body was rebelling and trying to keep me from speaking.
It was in June of 1981, shortly after I resigned as press secretary,
when I was invited to deliver a paper at a briefing seminar for the
Commission on Wartime Relocation and Internment of Civilians,
a body created by Congress to investigate the incarceration of Japanese Americans during World War II.

Even before my testimony I began to feel a constriction in my chest. During my testimony I had to grip the podium to keep myself from breaking down in tears. My chest tightened and it took all the strength I had to get my words out. My voice was hoarse and hardly recognizable. The severity of my emotional reaction was a mystery to me and it made me uneasy, for it was becoming increasingly apparent to me that there were forces residing in me that I was not aware of and that were beyond my control.

When I examined what I said to the commission and tried to extract the essence of what caused such violent emotional reaction within me, it boiled down to the implied statement, "I am Japanese." The core of my testimony was an incident at the Gila River Relocation Center where, while watching a war movie together with my friends, I cheered and applauded the sinking of a Japanese battleship. After describing the incident to the commission, I told them that it still filled me with shame: for it was an expression of hatred for the Japanese and, in effect, an expression of self-hatred. I said it was not difficult for me to understand the Black militancy of the 1960s. I could easily understand how a Black man might want to assert his own human dignity, and not see himself, as Franz Fanon said, through the eyes of his oppressor. For Japanese Americans, our incarceration, based solely on our race, was making us see ourselves through the eyes of our oppressor, white America. We were cheering the sight of a Japanese ship being bombed and its crew leaping for their lives into the ocean.

Later, when the commission held public hearings in several cities, hundreds of Japanese came forth to testify and the usually reserved and undemonstrative nisei choked back tears or let them flow as they told their stories. Younger Japanese in the audience were amazed to see people of their parents' generation becoming so emotional. "I never saw nisei act that way before," one of them said. Many considered those hearings the most important event in the life of the Japanese American community since the camps. It was as if an entire community was finally mourning its past and revealing its true feelings for the first time in forty years.

I wanted to capture those emotions in my book, but I found I could not do it. Although I was making some progress in dredging up old memories and feelings, I still did not clearly understand those emotions that were welling up in me and in other Japanese of my generation. Then, in 1982, I got help from an unexpected quarter. *National Geographic* offered me a contract to write an article on Japanese in America. The editors at the magazine had read a story I had written for *The Baltimore Sun* on the fortieth anniversary of President Roosevelt signing Executive Order 9066—the act that authorized the internment of Japanese in 1942. I had rewritten my testimony before the congressional commission as a newspaper article for the Sunday Perspective section of the paper.

Although the editors at *National Geographic* had not specified what sort of an article they were looking for, it was my impression that they wanted me to flesh out what social scientists have been saying for years, namely that Japanese Americans are an extraordinarily successful ethnic group, in fact a "model minority." I traveled to New York, Chicago, Los Angeles, San Francisco, Seattle, and Honolulu and interviewed more than a hundred Japanese of all ages and in a wide variety of occupations. At first I looked for success stories: a multimillionaire, lawyers working in white firms, a television anchor person, a rock band leader. But after a short while, I was no longer interested in writing about a model minority. I was not interested in writing at all. I wanted only to talk and listen to other Japanese.

In New York I met Takeru Iijima, a retired music teacher, who was a first sergeant in the all-nisei 442nd Regimental Combat Team. He was drafted on December 4, 1941, just three days before the attack on Pearl Harbor. After that, he said, the Army didn't know what to do with him and he was transferred from one camp to another and given menial assignments until the 442nd was formed. He said there might have been others who wanted to prove they were loyal Americans, but he did not think he had anything to prove. "I wanted to survive and get back home. That was the only thing on my mind." He did survive the fighting in Europe and returned home to New York. He got a degree in music education but could not get a teaching job even though there were jobs available. He worked as an unskilled laborer for four years until finally in 1950, he got a teaching job at a school in the South Bronx. "The principal took me only out of desperation," he said. "Nobody wanted to go there." When he retired 26 years later, he was chairman of the music department at the Thomas Jefferson High School in Brooklyn, but he was bitter about his wartime experience and the prejudice he faced after his return from the Army. "If I had to do it all over again," he said, "I'd say, 'Hell no.'"

I talked to his son Chris who, while attending Columbia University in the 1960s, engaged in anti-war demonstrations. While he was on the street shouting, "Hell no, we won't go," he said, it was inconceivable to him that his father was in the 442nd. "It was galling to me until I finally understood what they were trying to do," he said. It was the anti-war movement that got him interested in Japanese American history and the history of other non-white people. "For me, it was a revelation," he said. "It was the turning point of my life. I began to identify more with the Vietnamese than with the American soldiers. I began to identify with Puerto Ricans, the Blacks, and other Asian Americans." He said he also began to understand Japanese Americans of his father's generation. "They had a gun to their head."

I talked to Grant Ujifusa, a Harvard-educated, third-generation Japanese, who was working in New York as an editor for a large book publishing house. He was originally from Worland, Wyoming, where his grandparents had settled, so he and his family had been spared the camps. But he said he had an image of the "hypothetical trauma." He would not have had personal recollections of the camps because he was an infant at the time, but he said, "It would have scarred me. I would have experienced it later, when I was four, when I was ten. It would have been part of my life. It would have flowed in my veins as it has for most Japanese Americans.... If you cut my family off at the knee, you cut me off at the knees. My sense of manhood comes from my grandfather and father. If you emasculate them, you emasculate me."

In Los Angeles, I looked up Dan Kuramoto, the leader of the Hiroshima rock band, which used a mixture of western and Japanese instruments. While clearly western, the music the band played had traces of Japanese rhythms and melodies. I found Kuramoto, a third-generation Japanese American, to be a shy, soft-spoken man. During our conversation, I told him about my discomfort with seeing Japanese in groups, and he said he felt the same way. He said that he, too, had not come to terms with his own race and that performing on stage with other Japanese, using Japanese instruments and naming the group Hiroshima, was his way of combating his inherent timidity. He resembled a man who becomes a lion tamer to conquer a fear of lions. "It's my way of meeting a difficult issue head-on," he said.

Seeing my own nisei generation from across generational lines helped me. The third-generation sansei gave me hope, for they were so much further along than nisei in figuring out the Japanese American puzzle: what's wrong with us? Why are we so fearful? Dwight Chuman, a sansei journalist in Los Angeles, called the nisei of the 1940s "confused young men, who succeeded by selling their self-hatred and disappearing in the mainstream mentality." He referred to the model minority image, "The Quiet American," the smiling, hard-working, reliable professional Mr. Nice Guy. He made me think of how hakujin, upon meeting me, would often ask whether I knew a certain Japanese American acquaintance of theirs. "You happen to know George...?" a man would say. "A real nice guy." It seemed to me that we were all nice guys and it would be a relief for me to find a nisei who was mean, ornery, loud-mouthed, dishonest, and unreliable.

Amy Iwasaki Mass, a nisei clinical social worker, was six years old when she was sent with her family in the camp at Heart

Mountain, Wyoming. She said for years she remembered the internment as a "fun" experience and it was only in psychoanalysis that her true feelings came pouring forth. In working as a therapist with other nisei, she said, she discovered that they, too, had repressed much of their feelings surrounding the experience. Repression, she said, was our means of protecting ourselves from the frightening realization that our government was acting against us. The pleasant, non-offensive manners of most nisei, their neat grooming and appearance, their exaggerated concern or surface qualities are largely protective coloration, she said.

One sansei told me when he went to Japan, he was delighted to see that there were all kinds of Japanese: quiet and shy, loud and aggressive, polite, rude. "The Japanese of Japan have the whole range of human behavior through which they express themselves," he said. "We here in America confine ourselves to only a narrow band in the spectrum." I recalled from my childhood that my father and his issei friends were a hard-drinking, fun-loving group. They played as hard as they worked and individually they had distinctive personalities. Not all of them were honest or thoroughly reliable. As a group they contrasted sharply with their comparatively quiet, meek, and bland nisei children. World War II was an economic catastrophe for the issei and most of them never recovered from it. But for most issei, the war did not present any conflicts of loyalty and it did not seem to affect how they felt about themselves. The issei I talked to said their greatest worry was survival. Many Japanese who were employed by whites lost their jobs when the war broke out and were without any means of support. And when the "evacuation" began, some feared they were being sent to extermination camps. It came as an enormous relief to them that instead of being killed they were provided with food and shelter.

Their feelings about the political aspect of the war were in most cases clear. Shosuke Sasaki, an American-educated issei who lived in Seattle, said: "I felt the United States had been prodding Japan and succeeded in forcing Japan to fire the first shot. I was saddened because Japan was industrially not able to fight a country of the size of the United States, and stood a good chance of being crushed. I didn't blame the Japanese... Japan was on its knees for some kind of settlement from this country, but this country's only response was to spit on us. While I was saddened, I felt a certain pride that Japan refused to be bullied and insulted any longer." Sasaki was contemptuous of the Japanese American Citizens League, which cooperated with the wartime internment of Japanese. "They got down on all fours and licked the white man's boots with eagerness," he said.

Other issei I interviewed were not as harsh with the United States or with the Japanese American Citizens League as Sasaki, but none of them expressed any shame or guilt concerning the war or any lingering fears. The psychological trauma from the war appeared to have been sustained mainly by the nisei. Bebe Toshiko Reschke, a nisei psychiatric caseworker in Hollywood, California, was a child during the war, but she recalled that while in camp three military policemen came into her family's compartment to search for contraband. "I had such a feeling of being violated," she said. "I still have a problem with that, of trusting authority.... That anyone can have such control over you and it can happen so fast. When I read these negative stories dealing with Japan, I still get that emotional reaction. I think, 'Oh my God, the American public is turning against us again.' This time I'm not going. That's my line. This time I'm going to fight. I've joined the American Civil Liberties Union. That's my way of coping with my fears about what happened."

I had not wanted to visit the sites of any of the camps. But finally my editor at *National Geographic* convinced me that I should try to find the former site of the Gila River Relocation Center. I was glad when Sabine offered to go with me for it was becoming clearer to me that I was afraid of going to Gila. I saw myself wandering around in the desert in a Land Rover miles away from civilization.

I had tried to rent a four-wheel drive vehicle, but when we got to Phoenix none were available. I had made sure to bring along a pocketknife. It might be needed to cut open a snake bite. I made a mental note to buy a six-pack of Cokes to put in the trunk of the car. It would keep us going for a while if we got lost in the desert. When we got to our hotel, my chest was congested and I knew I was coming down with a case of bronchitis. It was going to be a race. I had to get to the camp site before the disease put me in bed. I called my brother, Nimashi, who lived in Phoenix, and he said he wanted to see the camp site, too. He had been living in Phoenix for nearly forty years and had not once visited the site, but he said he knew somebody who could give us directions.

We met Nimashi and his wife Sadako for breakfast. I had seen Nimashi only a few times after the war. At seventy, he was still working as a gardener. He was slim and bronzed by the sun and looked fit. The camp site, we later found, was only about thirty miles south of Phoenix and the Phoenix-to-Tucson expressway went within a few miles of it. But we had to take a roundabout route because first we had to visit a Mr. Ikeda to get directions. Mr. Ikeda had been living in the Phoenix at the time we were herded into the Gila camp. I remembered forty years earlier look-ing out of the train window and seeing the red-tiled houses shaded by palm trees and hoping that we would live in one of them. There had been Japanese living in such houses in Phoenix at the time and Mr. Ikeda was one of them. He had apparently gone to the site many times and was able to give us good directions.

We drove through the town of Chandler, whose name sounded familiar but I did not remember ever seeing before, and entered the Gila River Indian Reservation. There were irrigation ditches on both sides of the road and fields of lettuce, alfalfa, and grain. There were two camps at Gila, one called Canal and the other Butte. We had some difficulty finding the site of the Butte camp, the one we had been in, but we were able to determine its loca-tion by the concrete foundation blocks that were scattered about and the large slabs of concrete which were once the floors of mess halls. The sagebrush had spread again into the camp grounds and had grown up to seven feet tall. We walked around and looked. None of us had much to say.

The next day, Sabine and I returned to the site. My chest was better so we went to the top of the butte I had often climbed as a child. I showed Sabine the spot where Goro and I sat when he explained to me why the people in China were not upside down. From the top of the butte we could see green squares of cultivated fields. There was a cattle ranch nearby and we could see a man on horseback driving a few steers. There had been nothing but desert wilderness as far as the eye could see when I was a child. I felt high indignation that they were ruining my beautiful desert. I realized then that I had loved Gila. During the first weeks, I had been afraid of the desert, but as I became accustomed to my new surroundings, it was not Gila I feared, but rather the world outside—the world from which we had been ejected.

I began to realize that fear had never left me and that it had haunted me all my life. Why had I shouted at that reporter who had wanted to question that governor? It was because he had made me afraid. He had taken out his notebook and, for some inexplicable reason, was writing down every word I was saying. He was, in effect, accusing me of being a treacherous person who would connive with the governor to deceive the press and the public. In 1942, white authorities conceded that not all Japanese Americans were disloyal, but there was no way, they said, to weed out the disloyal from the loyal. The stereotype of the inscrutable Oriental was so deeply imbedded in the western mind that no one seriously questioned it. We were, therefore, all suspect and we were all removed from our homes and put in concentration camps.

When I sat down, finally, to write, I could not write the article I had set out to do: an upbeat story of a plucky group of Asian Americans who, having overcome a hard and bitter past, were the Horatio Algiers of our time. There was much evidence and material to support such a success story and it could have been written, but not by me. It would have deflected from the bitterness of the Japanese American experience. I could not paint a happy face on the Japanese American community when so many of us, especially the nisei, remained emotionally sick or crippled. Ultimately, *National Geographic* rejected my article, which dealt almost exclusively with the mass incarceration and its psychological aftermath. *The New York Times Magazine* later published an abridged version with the title, "The Anxiety of Being a Japanese American."

When I talked to Grant Ujifusa, the sansei editor, he told me his grandfather was delighted when the Heart Mountain Relocation Center was opened and thousands of Japanese came to Wyoming. He went frequently to the camp, where he could at long last mingle with his own people. I had a similar emotional experience when I traveled around the country seeking out Japanese. It was like an extension of my trip to Japan, where my cousins accepted me immediately as part of the family. I saw that we were indeed a people, with our own personality, character, history, and racial memory, and that our roots ran deep and were tenacious. In the Japanese I talked to, I saw myself. It was like a homecoming.

19

When I first went to *The Baltimore Sun*, I wrote a piece commemorating the twentieth anniversary of the ending of World War II,
which described the incarceration of Japanese Americans. The
main character in the piece was a boy named Hiroshi, a quasi-fic-
tional character who later became the protagonist in my attempt
at writing a novel. Two years later, in 1967, when *West Magazine* of
The Los Angeles Times asked me to write an article I insisted that the
experience be seen through the eyes of Hiroshi. The editor at *West
Magazine* was puzzled by that, but he agreed and the magazine
published the article with the title, "Remember Pearl Harbor, and
then...."

Hiroshi let me write in the third person and sustain the illusion that I was not writing about my own experiences, my own
feelings, but those of this imaginary and therefore invulnerable
child. I had to set Hiroshi aside, however, when I was asked in
1981 to deliver a briefing paper to the Commission on the Wartime
Relocation and Internment of Civilians. The commission wanted a
personal account of the experience, so I wrote for the first time in

the first person. It was more traumatic than I could have imagined. It took all my strength to keep myself from breaking down as I stood before the commission reading my paper whose principal point was that I was Japanese. I am an American, but an American of the Japanese race. That sentence would have struck me at one time as a contradiction in terms. I had become so used to accommodating the racist attitudes of my fellow Americans that I had become an anti-Japanese racist myself. World War II and my imprisonment offered only a partial explanation, and, if left unexamined, provided no resolution. I needed to look at them not as history, but as events that affected my life and my thoughts. I needed to try and relive my childhood and to rekindle old feelings to see what it was in the past that made the present seem so dark and threatening. What was it that made me so afraid, so ashamed, and feel so guilty?

Because of the stories my mother had read to me as a child and those my father told, it was my impression that Japanese history was extraordinarily violent and bloody. It appeared to have been a common practice for warriors to cut off the heads of those they defeated, especially if the vanquished were of high rank, and carry them back as proof of their valor. In my imagination I saw fields strewn with headless bodies trampled by fierce samurai with their bloody trophies swinging from their belts. It was a relief to me to read Winston Churchill's *History of the English-Speaking Peoples*, in which he described the mass slaughter that took place in the battles on the British Isles. The English, The Scots, and the Irish were every bit as barbaric as the Japanese.

When I read Japanese history, it struck me that, compared to Europe and the United States, it was remarkably peaceful. Medieval Japan had been racked by civil strife with warring clans vying for supremacy, but there were also periods of stability and relative calm. After Tokugawa Ieyasu unified the country in the early seventeenth century, Japan enjoyed peace and stability that lasted for two-and-a-half centuries. My mother was right. He was a great man. Compared to U.S. history, in which hardly thirty years go by without a major war, Tokugawa Japan was, despite its peasant uprisings, an island of tranquility.

It was more difficult for me to deal with modern Japanese history. Japanese aggression against China troubled me. Japan was behaving just as badly as the European powers, if not worse. There was no justification for the atrocities committed by Japanese troops. I read about the mass murders, the rapes and pillaging in Nanking, and the "death march of Bataan," desperately looking for extenuating circumstances, or at least some explanation for the barbaric behavior and savagery of the Japanese troops. I could not find any that satisfied me.

When I was writing about ethnic affairs at *The Sun*, I did a story on the foreign Islamic community in Baltimore. While researching the piece I met a Pakistani who asked me whether I was Buddhist. I replied I was at most a nominal Buddhist. My parents were Buddhist so that might make me one, but I had never practiced the religion as an adult. He then asked me whether Buddhists revered life in all forms I replied that is what I had read, but I didn't know much about it. Then the man, who seemed to be getting angrier and angrier, said Buddhists in Burma a few years earlier had massacred hundreds of Muslims and he asked how that squared with a reverence for life. He railed at me saying that Buddhists were hypocrites and glared as if he expected me to defend the actions of the Burmese Buddhists or perhaps apologize for them. I, of course, could do neither, but the man made me feel guilty. I pondered this feeling of guilt, which seemed to defy all reason, and it ultimately helped me. I began to realize that I did not need to defend or apologize for the evil deeds committed by the Japanese. The Japanese were capable of evil because they were human, and human beings of every race have committed unspeakably cruel and violent acts throughout history. If there were within me the seeds of evil, they were there because I was human. And being human, there was also within me the capacity for goodness. I was as free to choose between good and evil as anybody else and my race was no cause for shame or despair.

I saw, at last, not just the injustice of our being imprisoned during World War II, but the absurdity of it. Just as the Pakistani needed to upbraid me for the actions of the Burmese Buddhists, the American public and the American government needed to take some action against Japanese living in the United States after the attack on Pearl Harbor. When they heard reports of the atrocities committed by Japanese troops against American soldiers in the Philippines, there was an even stronger urge to act. If national security were the issue, there was more reason to imprison the Japanese in Hawaii, which had been shown to be vulnerable to attack by Japanese naval forces. But there was no mass incarceration of Japanese there because they constituted a third of the population and a third of the work force. The Japanese on the mainland were expendable and could be made scapegoats. The American people and government faced a national crisis and there was an overpowering need to lash out, to do something—anything. And so, because a jap was a jap, the government rounded up Japanese Americans.

The knowledge that the camps had been based on racism and wartime hysteria was not enough to dispel my feelings of shame and guilt. During the war I began to share the anti-Japanese feelings. But I was not angry like other Americans about Pearl Harbor; I felt guilty instead. And when I heard about the atrocities committed by Japanese troops, I was ashamed and felt guilty about that as well. We ought to have been imprisoned. I, too, wanted action, vengeance. It was the Stockholm syndrome: I, the captive, had taken on the point of view of my captor. But can one wreak vengeance against oneself?

I tried to kill the Japanese in me, to submerge myself deeper and deeper into the white world. For many years, it worked; I could succeed and be accepted in a white society. So complete was my psychic submersion at times that when I looked in the mirror

I would be surprised to see a Japanese staring back at me. At other times, I felt like an actor on a stage. None of my accomplishments had much meaning for me because they were not my accomplishments, they were those of the characters I had played or was currently playing. I could be equally detached from my failures. Even the thought of suicide and death did not hold the usual terror for me. I could not kill somebody who was not really there, who had not been there for a very long time.

It is often said that time heals all wounds. But some wounds fester subcutaneously even after all outward signs are gone. The Greek tragedians knew that, for what else is a curse that follows a family for generations, but a metaphor for the festering effects of an offense that cannot be forgiven or a hurt that will not be healed. There are times when a wound must be opened and cleansed no matter how painful the process.

While in the Army I read an essay by Alfred North Whitehead, in which he said, "The present contains all that there is. It is holy ground; for it is the past and it is the future." The thought intrigued me and it has stayed with me. What it has come to mean to me is that we carry with us our own reality which shifts and grows and at times retreats, but which at any given moment defines who we are. It is not necessarily true that we are the sum of all our experiences, for we are capable of shrinking our minds and hearts to become less than what we are or are capable of being. That is what I had done and a great many other Japanese in America have done. The bombs that fell on Pearl Harbor on December 7, 1941, set off a chain of events that set me adrift from my past—my parents, my family, and my childhood. I was cut off from that child within me that is the core of my being. I have named that child Hiroshi and in an attempt to find him I have tried writing about him in fiction and nonfiction, but he has remained elusive.

When I first began writing about Hiroshi, around 1965, I did so because I felt I had been cut in half by the war. It seemed to me that my American half survived, but my Japanese half shriveled and died. Hiroshi was the last image I had of the whole child. He was the child who ate misoshiru and shouted "banzai!" to the emperor on his birthday, listened to the Lone Ranger on radio, and followed the adventures of Batman in the comic books. He was neither American nor Japanese, but simply me. I thought I had found him when I visited Japan as a young man of 27 but concluded before I left that Yoshitaka-san was a caricature, a distorted, one-dimensional view of Hiroshi. I saw Hiroshi's shadow when I visited Guadalupe in 1983, but nothing more. I got a glimpse of him in the desert wilderness of Arizona when I visited Gila the following year. Sometimes I see him vaguely, very vaguely, in my children. Where I need to see him is within myself. This book was intended to clear away the fear and confusion that have attended my search for Hiroshi. I needed to determine when and where I had lost him for the search to continue.

EPILOGUE

Throughout my life, whenever I felt lost and in deep despair, I would find myself saying, "I want to go home." But where and what was that? When in 1983 I visited Guadalupe, my hometown in rural California, it looked physically as I remembered it. Main Street and most of the buildings I remembered were still there. But I saw no Japanese standing on the street, no clutter of Japanese-owned shops and businesses. It was not the street my friends and I walked to school on, nor the one we roller-skated on to the annoyance of shopkeepers who indulged us because they knew us and our parents. What had made Guadalupe my home was a sense of belonging and a feeling of being safe and secure. That it had taken me so long to arrive at that simple understanding was an indication of how deep the trauma of World War II, the mass imprisonment, the shattering of my family and childhood had been.

White people whose ancestors have lived multiple generations in the United States and even newer arrivals from Europe, only a generation or two removed from their countries of origin, have less difficulty identifying themselves and being seen by others as

Americans. It is more complicated with non-white people. Your race is not only the first thing others see about you, but a part of how you see yourself. Race can shape for better or for worse the course of your life beginning with childhood.

Over the decades that followed our imprisonment I had to find a new home and it was not anything like Guadalupe. It was America, a half a continent dominated by white people who needed to be told that it was also my home. Even today, as I assert that I am an American, my views on Americanism are probably different from those who've never been told that they don't belong.

In 1991 *Newsweek* asked me to write a piece for their issue commemorating the 50th anniversary of the Japanese attack on Pearl Harbor. When I wrote that in Japan the attack on Pearl Harbor was seen in the context of western imperialism, I got angry letters from readers who thought of the attack as simply an isolated and evil act of treachery.

In the early 1970s when I was assigned to *The Baltimore Sun*'s Washington Bureau, I was having a drink with my bureau chief, Phil Potter, at the Washington Press Club. When the conversation turned to the war years, Phil said, "Gene, what the government did to you was wrong, but some good came out of it. It got you out of your ghettos in the west and spread you around the country. It helped to get you assimilated into American society." Somewhere in the back of my mind I was offended by his words, but I was at a loss on how to respond. There I was standing at the bar of the Washington Press Club, where I was a member, having a drink with one of Washington's most distinguished journalists. Before the war, I would have been lucky to land a job as a waiter there. I ended up saying weakly, "Yeah, maybe you're right, Phil."

A decade later, when I visited Phil at his retirement home in California, he repeated, as old men will do, the very same opinion in virtually the same words. By that time, I had started exploring my childhood and writing about it, so I was able to defend the "ghetto" in which I grew up as a culturally vibrant and rich community, exposed to both Japanese and American languages, art, movies and history, that greatly expanded my understanding of the world beyond America.

The English poet William Wordsworth said there are two types of people in this world: those who had a happy childhood and those who did not. I had a happy childhood until December 7, 1941, when my world collapsed and turned into something I did not know. The happiness that preceded the war is what I had in mind when I named my memoir *In Search of Hiroshi*. I see now that the essential element of my happiness was the feeling of wholeness. I was simply myself at the time and did not have the burden of what W.E.B. Dubois called a "double consciousness." The burden placed on a Black man in Dubois' view is knowing himself as he is and at the same time having to see himself through the eyes of the white society in which he lives. In the same vein, Frantz Fanon, known for his blistering critiques of colonialism and slavery, writes of the devastating effect on the oppressed of having to see themselves through the eyes of their oppressors.

I believe all people of color have much to learn from Black historians and writers even if our racial memories and heritage are not pierced through with four centuries of slavery. I have benefitted from the writings and insights of Black writers and activists intellectually and in practical ways. I am convinced that I would not have been hired by the Associated Press in 1963 were it not for the great Civil Rights Movement of the 1950s and 60s.

Even after having attained a measure of professional success and social acceptance, however, I still had to adapt to how other Americans saw me: at first sight at least an Asian man who spoke English remarkably well. I experienced it as a legacy from the war. How could Americans see me as one of them after the sneak attack on Pearl Harbor and our mass incarceration. Even after our release I was still assailed by notions that there was something wrong with me, or with my parents, or with Japanese generally. I survived by acting as if I was no different than anybody else. As a teenager, to get past my strict Confucian upbringing, I smoked, drank, aspired to be a jazz musician and got high on pot. Fortunately, perhaps because of my upbringing, I was good in school and eventually made my way through college and graduate school, ending up in a white man's profession.

I began to understand the source of my troubles when I began to accept that I was different from most other Americans and that was something I had to learn to live with. Gradually, cautiously at first, I began to think seriously of what it meant to be Japanese. One important memory I have is a conversation that took place in 1963 when I was a graduate student in journalism at UCLA where I met a student from Korea. During one of our talks, he was surprised to find that I was mostly ignorant about the history of the Opium War fought by the British against the Chinese in the 1840s—a conflict often seen as the beginning of western domination of China and the downfall of the Chinese empire. "Gene," he said in a shocked tone, "you don't know your own history!" I was flattered that he accepted me as a fellow Asian despite the fraught relationship between Japan and Korea and the rest of Asia. In hindsight, it seems like the beginning of seeing myself, or more importantly, accepting myself at least in part as an Asian.

As it turned out, I was not only ignorant of Asian history, but the history of immigration to America as well. Contrary to the welcoming words inscribed on the Statue of Liberty, immigrants from Europe, especially Catholics, Jews and swarthy people from Southern and Eastern Europe faced formidable prejudice and political opposition. Hatred and even violence against Chinese were especially fierce and led to their exclusion in 1882, foreshadowing the ban on Japanese immigration 42 years later.

After the publication of In Search of Hiroshi, and during my retirement, I taught a series of courses in retirement communities on Asian history and philosophy. I had begun my study with Japanese history from prehistoric times to the attack on Pearl Harbor. When I discovered that virtually all Japanese culture originated in China, I read Chinese history as well as books on Chinese philosophy and religions. It was only then that I realized that my upbringing was based on Confucianism. Growing up in America, I could not help but be influenced by the Judeo-Christian ethic, but my moral underpinnings were founded on an ancient and revered Chinese philosophy. I was different from most other Americans, and I am now fine with that.

In Search of Hiroshi was my first serious attempt to understand how the totality of my childhood experiences, against the backdrop of the mid-20th century cultural and political environment, set a course for my life, my self-identity and thoughts. My family and I were put in a concentration camp for being of the Japanese race, but I did not hold it against America. Instead, I wondered what, if anything, was wrong with me. The realization that the United States was wrong in incarcerating me came slowly over period of decades. When Congress of the United States in 1988 enacted a resolution apologizing for our unconstitutional incarceration, it brought tears to my eyes. I am still moved whenever I come upon a reference to it.

In what my Swiss wife gently calls my narcissistic focus on myself, I had assumed earlier in our marriage that our children enjoyed a life free of racial concerns or antagonism. The ambiguities of their racial makeup apparently were not a barrier to having white friends and to their academic and professional success. It was only when they approached and entered adulthood that I learned from them their difficulties and struggles in growing up as mixed-race children, what we now jokingly call "stranger babies." I do not think, however, that they ever doubted their identity as Americans even when there were those around them who did. A multiracial society was beginning to emerge and they did not, like me, have to live life in what felt at times like a masquerade.

Today, I understand that The Search for Hiroshi was a search for myself and the totality of who I am—an American who was born and raised in a family and neighborhood steeped in the Japanese language and culture. That childhood enriched my life and did not make me less American than the children of the Irish, Italian, Jews and other immigrants from Europe. Now, deep into old age, I no longer feel a need to justify my own existence or my place in my country. The memoir ends with a suggestion that the search will continue. That was three decades ago, and in the meantime I have come to the realization that the child I called "Hiroshi" had never been lost. My memoir is not about the state of the world so much as my place in it.

With that narrow perspective much has changed, and Hiroshi in meaning and context is no longer the same. He consisted of memories deep and abiding that have lived within me throughout my life. What he had been for me was a nostalgic vision of my past unmoored from the present. He had also been my personal Pandora's box, full of dangerous memories, secrets and fears, which, as it turned out, only needed to be set free.

REFLECTIONS

I.

GILA RIVER REVISITED:
TWO GENERATIONS REMEMBER
by Eve Oishi & Gene Oishi

II.

A (YONSEI) EDITOR'S NOTE:
SEEING OURSELVES ACROSS GENERATIONAL LINES
by Ana Iwataki

GILA RIVER REVISTED:

TWO GENERATIONS REMEMBER

EVE OISHI & GENE OISHI

Below is a talk that my father and I gave at the Association of Asian American Studies conference in Scottsdale, Arizona on May 27, 2000. When we learned that the 2000 conference was going to be held in Arizona and would include a group tour to the nearby site of the Gila River incarceration camp, we decided to turn the event into an opportunity to reflect on the lasting effect my father's imprisonment during WWII has had on our family. We wrote the first part of the paper before we went to Arizona, exchanging drafts and building our writing in response to each other's work. Two days before our presentation, we visited the site together. Located on the Gila River Indian Reservation, the site had been preserved as a monument by the Gila River Indian Community (GRIC), and it sat rather forlornly amid acreage that was primarily leased for farming. Returning to our hotel rooms afterwards, we wrote the final sections of this essay. The rest of our family—my mother, my siblings and their spouses—attended the talk and visited the Gila River site with the rest of the tour the next day.

As it accompanies the re-publication of my father's 1988 memoir, we are publishing this talk with only minor edits as a document of our intergenerational conversation over two decades ago. It is remarkable, for example, how completely terms like "relocation" and "internment," which were standard at the time of our original talk, have been replaced by "incarceration" and "imprisonment" both in the scholarly literature and in our own personal vocabularies. Just over a year after giving this talk, when the Twin Towers fell in New York, my father wrote and spoke widely about the parallels he was seeing between his own childhood experiences and the racialized surveillance and incarceration of Muslims being carried out in the name of national security. The activism of police and prison abolitionists, finally entering mainstream discourse after the 2020 police murders of Breonna Taylor and George Floyd, has provided frameworks for connecting histories of carcerality in the U.S. among and across populations and across histories of enslavement, enclosure, and dispossession.

The political and academic work on settler colonialism, including the positioning of Asian settlers, has helped to unearth and clarify the complex historical entanglement between the original inhabitants of Gila River Indian Community—the Akimel O'otham (Pima) and Pee-Posh peoples (Maricopa)—and the Japanese Americans who were incarcerated on their land from 1942 until 1945. As Karen J. Leong and Myla Vicenti Carpio write in 2016 special issue of Amerasia Journal on Indigenous and Asian experiences in the Americas, "[t]he forced relocation of Japanese Americans evoked carceral logics similar to those deployed by the federal government's actions against American Indians a century earlier."[1] In their article "Carceral Subjugations: Gila River Indian Community and Incarceration of Japanese Americans on Its Lands," Leong and Carpio recount the process by which Commissioner of Indian Affairs John Collier recommended Gila River to Secretary of the Interior Harold Ickes as one of several possible sites for the wartime camps with the idea of using Japanese American prisoner labor to develop tribal land "that the settler-induced lack of water had rendered infertile."[2] Gila River was chosen as the site for the camp with a plan for the prisoners to clear and irrigate almost 100,000 acres of "raw land,"[3] taking over agricultural projects that had been designed to support tribal self-sufficiency.

Leong and Carpio describe the ways in which this scheme relied upon ideas about Indigenous communities as unable to extract value from their lands and Japanese Americans as model minority agriculturalists who could make this land productive. Thus, the Japanese American prisoners were compelled to perform both agricultural and "cultural labor,"[4] as their reputation for agricultural productivity was employed to support the disenfranchisement of the Indigenous occupants under the logic that

---

[1] Leong, Karen J. & Carpio, Myla Vicenti, "Carceral Subjugations: Gila River Indian Community and Incarceration of Japanese Americans on Its Lands," *Amerasia Journal*, v. 42, no.1 (2016): 103-120, p. 107.

[2] Ibid, p. 109.

[3] Ibid, p. 109.

[4] Ibid, p. 114.

the best way to extract value from the land was to separate it from its original inhabitants. These logics obscured the fact that the Gila River Indian Community "had already undergone several years of clearing and plowing close to 10,000 acres of land, and planting alfalfa to enrich the soil." The incarcerated Japanese farmers, who could be paid "much lower than market WRA wage," were being brought in to continue a large-scale land improvement that had already been started by the GRIC.[5] Despite the original justification that this improvement would help to support GRIC self-sustainability by making the land productive and providing infrastructure, when the camp was closed, the WRA approved the removal of water pipes and electrical lines.[6] While the Department of the Interior had undermined community water rights before the war, it increased the water allotment to the land while the incarceration camps were in operation, and then reduced it again significantly when they were closed. Citing fear of "(non-Indian) water users," the WRA stopped cultivating the land after the war.[7] This entangled history shades and rearranges our jokes about tribal police as well as the ways that the landscape had been overtaken by settler farmland. The process of revisiting Gila River has deepened the nature of our family connections, but it has also clarified my family's positioning within interwoven and ever-expanding networks and histories of people and place.

Archaeologist Kenji Lau-Ozawa's work on the Gila River Incarceration Camp reinforces the idea that the particular history of the site as a prison camp requires researchers to employ different methods and rely on different forms of evidence to understand the lives of people imprisoned there. He uses inscriptions—names and initials carved into concrete or mentioned in the camp newspaper—and silences—the administrative and cultural elision of Okinawan and queer incarcerees within the historical record—as openings for more extensive historical excavation.[8] His focus on the gaps and silences in the archive, as well as his linking of the

---

[5] Ibid, p. 109.

[6] Ibid, p. 112.

[7] Ibid, p. 115.

[8] Lau-Ozawa, Koji, "Inscriptions and Silences: Challenges of Bearing Witness at the Gila River Incarceration Camp." *International Journal of Historical Archaeology*, vol. 25 no. 3 (2021): 851-876.

physical landscape of the camp with the memories and experiences of its inhabitants, helps to underscore the power of the physical site. Returning in memory to Gila River so many years later, I am reminded most strongly of the feeling of the sun and the smell of the dust, the way the ground rose and fell, and how the light changed throughout the day. Gila River is not simply a metaphor, but an actual place, whose environmental features contoured the experiences and memories of its human inhabitants and whose geological strata are shaped and marked by their brief presence.

Subsequent research on Japanese American incarceration has also some shed light on the Tule Lake "mystery stones" that I referred to in the talk. After the camp was closed and the land given away to homesteaders by the Bureau of Reclamation, Les and Nora Bovee, who had been awarded a parcel of land through a lottery, uncovered a 55-gallon oil drum that had been filled with over one thousand stones. Each stone was painted with a Chinese character. The Bovees kept the barrel in a barn and over the years many were taken or given away. In 1994 they donated the remaining 656 stones to the Japanese American National Museum. Eventually Japanese scholar Sodo Mori used a computer program to match the characters and the frequency with which they appear on the stones to the Lotus Sutra, one of the key sutras of the Nichiren Buddhist sect. Drawing on data from the Heart Mountain camp newspaper, Mori has hypothesized that the stones are, at least partly, the work of Heart Mountain internee and Buddhist priest Reverend Nichikan Murikata, created as a ritual of devotion during the years of incarceration.[9] The specific details of the authorship and motivation behind these stones still remains a mystery.

My academic journey began as a similar form of excavation, an attempt to trace the things that I knew and felt back to events from before I was born. When nisei elders met, they would often talk about "camp" in ways that felt like a code. The word evoked the carefree, rustic pleasures of summer vacation, yet they never discussed details, and the brevity of the conversations carried a sense of the illicit or the shameful. I was lucky to have a father who shared many details of his childhood, even if the shar-

---

[9] Russell, Dakota, "The Heart Mountain Mystery Stones: Buried in American Soil," https://500objects.org/object/the-heart-mountain-mystery-stones-2/

ing was part of a painful process of self-discovery that we were witness to. Going into academia was a logical extension of that quest to connect the present to the past, the urge to solve intriguing mysteries while at the same time understanding the larger context that will leave some questions forever unanswered. An ongoing theme of my work has been to understand why some people remember and others forget, why some people's memories are recorded and preserved, while others are not. The parts of the mystery we will never solve are, to me, the most beautiful.

EVE OISHI 2023

GENE OISHI: This paper deals with the internment of 110,000 persons of Japanese ancestry living in the United States after the outbreak of World War II. Of this group, 71,000, roughly two-thirds, were American citizens, or "non-aliens," as they were described in some official documents. I was nine years old at the time and one of the non-aliens.

On Thursday of this week my daughter Eve and I visited the site of the Gila River camp where my family and I were interned. It was my third visit to the site, and the first for my daughter, who is the co-author of this paper. It struck me again, as it did on my previous visits, that I was not unhappy in the camp. After the first year or so, the food supply became adequate. My friends and I played the usual childhood games, formed football and baseball teams, and explored the desert that was beautiful and fascinating. To be uprooted from one's home and to be herded into a concentration camp is a traumatic experience that doesn't require much explanation or imagination to understand. But what I realized upon revisiting the place of my incarceration, was that being released from the camp was as frightening as the original imprisonment. For I was leaving what I now saw as a safe and friendly environment and being thrust back into a hostile society that had ejected us and did not want us back.

The main focus of this paper therefore is not on the internment itself but on its aftermath. It examines: (1) how the experience has informed my view of myself and the society in which I live, and (2) the ways the imprisonment might have persisted into post-war years by keeping Japanese Americans in psychological and spiritual bondage to the majority culture.

EVE OISHI: This paper also addresses the lingering, often unspoken effects of the internment on the generations of Japanese Americans who were born after the war, but whose lives have been irrevocably shaped by the experience of internment. In her recent documentary film, *When You're Smiling: The Deadly Legacy of Internment*, Janice Tanaka explores the unreported toll taken by the internment on the sansei generation. She investigates a rash of mysterious deaths of sansei youth in the early 1970's (thirty-one in the year 1971 alone) and discovers that the deaths were the result of suicide or drug overdose. Many of the doctors' reports had been falsified to indicate other, less scandalous, causes of death.[10] According to her documentary, one of the deadliest legacies of the internment in the Japanese American community has been silence—the reluctance of the nisei generation to talk to their children about their experiences, and the conspiracy of silence around the presence of emotional distress, substance abuse, depression and mental illness within the Japanese American community.

Because of our ages, (born in 1932 and 1967), my father and I fall somewhat between traditional Japanese American generations—he is a young nisei who, educated at Berkeley in the 1960's, shares many experiences with the sansei generation. I, in turn, share many qualities and identifications with both the sansei generation (children who were born after the war but whose parents were in camp) and the younger yonsei generation. Perhaps this is why we have chosen to reach across generational lines—to break the silences about the internment that have choked families in the Japanese American community for over fifty years, to take a deeper look at some of the reasons for this silence and to invent new ways of speaking to each

---

[10] Tanaka, Janice, 1999, *When You're Smiling: The Deadly Legacy of Internment*. Visual Communications.

other about the nature and the possibilities of memory.

GO: I agree that there was something like "a conspiracy of silence" surrounding our wartime experience. One reason was a profound fear and sense of shame that the experience instilled in us, which I will address later in this paper. In the post-war years the discussion concerning the internment of Japanese Americans focused almost exclusively on relatively unemotional Constitutional issues. Nisei, Japanese Americans of my generation, were careful not to express anger or bitterness. And issues such as racial and cultural differences were avoided. Post-war critics of the internment understood that the more culturally "American" Japanese Americans were, the more unjustified their incarceration would appear to be to the general public. And conversely, the greater the cultural differences between Japanese Americans and the white majority, the less emotionally and even less legally convincing would be the charge that constitutional rights were flagrantly and needlessly violated.

At the time of the internment, however, the issue was defined by the government quite openly in racial and, by inference, cultural terms. Lieutenant General John D. DeWitt, commander of the Western Defense Command, recommended to the War Department that all persons of Japanese ancestry be removed from the West Coast of the United States because:

> In the war in which we are now engaged racial affinities are not severed by migration. The Japanese race is an enemy race and while many second and third generation Japanese, born on United States soil, possessed of United States citizenship, have become 'Americanized,' the racial strains are undiluted... It therefore follows that along the vital Pacific Coast over 112,000 potential enemies of Japanese extraction are at large today.[11]

The great civil rights movement was still decades away and Americans had not yet been forced to confront the racism that infused all

---

11 DeWitt, John Lesesne, *Final Report: Japanese Evacuation from the West Coast, 1942* (Washington: U.S. Government Printing Office, 1943)

facets of American life. The following quotations are from the 1942 Congressional Record:

Congressman John Rankin, Mississippi:
This is a race war, as far as the Pacific side of this conflict is concerned....The white man's civilization has come into conflict with Japanese barbarism....One of them must be destroyed.[12]

Sen. Tom Stewart, Tennessee:
The Japanese are among our worst enemies. They are cowardly and immoral. They are different from Americans in every conceivable way, and no Japanese should have a right to claim American citizenship. A Jap is a Jap anywhere you find him and his taking the oath of allegiance to this country would not help, even if he is permitted to do so. They don't believe in God and have no respect for an oath.[13]

To be sure, these are Southerners, not known for racial tolerance in those days. But here is what Henry McLemore, a columnist for the Hearst papers, wrote:

I am for immediate removal of every Japanese on the West Coast to a point deep in the interior. I don't mean a nice part of the interior either. Herd 'em up, pack 'em off and give' em the inside room in the badlands. Let 'em be pinched, hurt, hungry and dead up against it....Personally, I hate the Japanese. And that goes for all of them.[14]

Minorities in America, people of color in particular, have always known the dangers associated with being different. But during World War II Japanese Americans as a group learned in a stark, catastrophic way the dangers that attend racial and cultural differences. Among the first to be arrested after the bombing of Pearl Harbor

---

[12] *Congressional Record*, December 15, 1941, p. 9808.

[13] *Congressional Record*, February 26, 1942, pp. 1682-1683.

[14] McLemore, Henry, *San Francisco Examiner*, January 20, 1942.

were community leaders, Japanese language teachers and Buddhist priests. If it was dangerous to be culturally different, it was even more dangerous to be a leader or a teacher in a culturally diverse community. The FBI arrested my father the night of Pearl Harbor because he was prominent in the Japanese community and his pro-Japanese sentiments were well known. Because he was not of a white race, he was ineligible for American citizenship and he made no secret of the strong affinity he felt for the land of his birth.[15]

EO: The idea that visibility equals vulnerability was something that was bred into me as a third generation Japanese American. I have always known that there is such a thing as cultural memory, a deep-seated knowledge that is inherited and passed down from one generation to the next; but in order to understand how this transmission works, one has to look at family histories, dynamics and patterns. In his book, *In Search of Hiroshi*, my father wrote, "After the war, I tried to get as far a possible away from my Japanese background, but not without sorrow and a sense of loss."[16] As mine was the only Asian family I knew in Baltimore, Maryland, a city that was overwhelmingly white and black, and as I was the child of a Japanese American father and a European mother, my experience of home, my very identity, was a symbol of my father's distance from the Japanese American community, from his own racial status. Although we were much more familiar with our mother's family in Switzerland, both of my parents had chosen to live thousands of miles from their family and culture. My mother, whose father was Swiss and whose mother was a German Jew who escaped Nazi Germany just before the war, also describes a childhood in which she never felt completely a part of her culture.

I grew up with the unacknowledged sense that we were in hiding, a kind of cultural witness protection program. It was very

---

[15] Since the Naturalization Law of 1790, only "whites" were eligible for naturalized citizenship. Although the category of "whites" was revised several times, and Asians brought numerous legal challenges to this restriction, Japanese immigrants were not allowed to become naturalized citizens until the McCarran-Walter Act of 1952.

[16] Oishi, Gene, *In Search of Hiroshi* (Rutland, VT and Tokyo: Charles E. Tuttle Company, 1988): 10.

important to show a certain face to the outside world, to not make trouble, to be a model citizen. As very young children, my sister and I prided ourselves on our stoicism at the doctor's office, how we, unlike the other screaming American children, could take medicine and shots without a flinch or a whimper. My parents have often remarked on how fearful we were. When we would go out to a restaurant for dinner, we would ask our parents if they had enough money to pay for the meal. One of their twisted parent games was to pretend that they didn't have enough money to pay the bill. They were amazed at how consistently and predictably we would fall for it, going into a panic about how we would manage to pay for our meal, what the consequences would be for our crime. At the time, no one made the connection to our parents' histories, but the question haunts me today. Where did we get it: that feeling that they could come for us at any time? That we needed to behave, to assimilate, to become invisible in order to escape the ever-present threat of detection and of punishment.

Years after my father left his most public job, as press secretary for the governor of Maryland, we talked about what a difficult experience it was for him to be so visible. What began as a painful revelation has gradually evolved into something of a family in-joke. We could always tell when he was on the phone with reporters because he would be using his "hakujin voice." The qualities of "whiteness" (hakujin) that we identified in his voice were a carefulness, a brittleness, the use of perfect grammar and modulation as a defense, a shield of invisibility. I hear that voice come out of my mouth whenever I am feeling vulnerable, when I have to address deans, landlords, the IRS, anyone who might have power over me. My early sense of what my Japanese identity meant was abstract: something to be protected, something inherently vulnerable, something to be kept in the family. Now I realize that this was more than the neurotic tendencies of a high-strung child; it was the legacy of a particular community of families. It was the link between me and a larger history that we needed to revisit together.

GO: During our internment, one of my brothers volunteered for the Army and another was drafted after they responded affirmatively to an U.S. loyalty questionnaire. I was a child, so nobody asked me where my loyalty lay. It was a good thing, because I was not sure. In camp we saw war movies that showed Japanese pilots laughing as they machine gunned Americans parachuting out of their burning planes. We saw Japanese soldiers bayoneting wounded GIs. And when the Marines finally landed and started killing the Japanese, my friends and I cheered. But I felt badly about it. Perhaps if I were truly a loyal American I would not have had any qualms, but I can confess today that I did not like seeing Japanese killed. After the war, people would ask me if I were angry or bitter about the internment. I said I was neither, but could not explain. The real issue was not how I felt about the government, but how I felt about myself. When my father was arrested, I thought I did not want to see him again. The government did not ask me to disown my father, but it was my impression that to be a true American, you had to hate Japanese. How then was it possible to be an American of the Japanese race?

In 1991 *Newsweek* magazine asked me to write an article giving my thoughts as a Japanese American for a special issue commemorating the fiftieth anniversary of the attack on Pearl Harbor. I quote from the first paragraph of the article:

> *I call myself an American of the Japanese race, a formulation that used to strike many Americans as a contradiction in terms. Because of the perceived paradox in our identity, Japanese Americans tend to downplay, even deny, their Japanese half, insisting we are as American as anyone else. I will not argue that point one way or another. What I do wish to assert, however, is that I am different from most Americans. I have always felt, and still feel today, a kinship with Japan, the country where both my parents were born.*[17]

I think some Japanese Americans of my generation winced at reading my article. For a Japanese American to admit he felt an affinity for Japan would seem to justify our internment. But that is only a guess because neither *Newsweek* nor I got any letters from Japanese

---

[17] Oishi, Gene, "Our Neighbors Called Us Japs," *Newsweek*, November 25, 1991.

Americans. Those who did write were people out of the past. They could not or would not understand that I was writing my article as an American. For them, an American of the Japanese race remained a contradiction in terms. They questioned my honesty and motives and wanted to show that they saw through my Oriental deviousness. They saw my article as Japanese propaganda, even though it was written a half-century after the attack on Pearl Harbor by an individual who was but a child when the event took place. Time has stood still for them, as time will for victims of great catastrophes. Time has stood still for me and other Japanese Americans as well.

EO: When I was five years old, my family moved to West Germany where my father had a post as a foreign correspondent for *The Baltimore Sun*. In 1972, West Germany was just beginning to wrestle with the growing presence of immigrants and *Gastarbeiters*, but three brown children were still a fairly rare sight in most suburban neighborhoods. Although, for most of my education, I did not attend German schools, the reaction of the average German child on the street to us was one of unabashed racism, mockery and often the threat of violence. While these incidents were a part of my daily life, it was not particularly traumatizing for me. It was unpleasant, certainly embarrassing, but not more than that. Even though we lived in Germany for four years, I never thought of it as my home. I always knew that I would return to my home, America, and I carried with myself (perhaps developed as a mechanism of defense) a fundamental but unspoken sense of myself as American. These early childhood experiences with racism were, as I said, unpleasant, but they were one of the tiresome but unavoidable experiences of the tourist, the expatriate, more a sign of the intolerance of German society than any reflection on myself.

This attitude would be greatly challenged when I returned to the U.S. at the age of nine, the same age as my father when he left his home in California for a camp in Arizona. Coming back to school in the States, I encountered the usual schoolyard racism—the "ching chong" taunts, the fingers pulling eyes to slits—and I found myself momentarily thrown off-balance. This I was not expecting. The stance I had previously relied on—that these were not my people, that this was not my home—no longer worked. I learned in that very American year—it was, after all, the Bicentennial—that I was both fundamentally, inescapably American and that, because of my race, I would never really be American. This is, in many ways, the essential nature of American culture: it defines you completely even as you can never be completely American if you are part of a minority. But this experience also shaped my experiences and ideas of home. As a person of color, biracial, living abroad, I learned that home is both a place in your consciousness—a place of enormous psychic and emotional importance—as well as a shifting, unstable place, one that can only exist elsewhere. Years later, when I spent a year in Japan after college, this lesson was once again confirmed. I was drawn there from a sense of historical belonging. I had never felt fully American, so perhaps I would find some sense of home in Japan. The unexpected, uneasy, comforting lesson I learned that year was how deeply American I am. It is an identity, a home that I can only fully experience when I am away from it.

In 1982 my father, on assignment for *National Geographic* magazine, returned to Gila River for the first time, bringing with him my mother and my younger brother. In his account, which was eventually published in the *New York Times Magazine*, he described his fear of returning to the site of internment, the source of so much of his psychological and emotional turmoil.[18] When he reached the site, however, he was surprised to find that his reaction was not one of pain and emotional breakdown, but a warm and nostalgic familiarity. His only unpleasant reaction was to how much the site had changed. Much of the desert had been irrigated and had been turned into farmland, and it disturbed him that the view was not exactly the same as it had been when he was a child. The memories of trauma, of fear and alienation, he realized, were not associated with camp; they were associated with leaving camp and returning to a hostile outside world that had authorized, demanded, or at least allowed them to be sent away to prison. In many ways, our family's various exiles—in Germany, in Baltimore—represented a similar ex-

---

[18] Oishi, Gene, "The Anxiety of Being Japanese-American" *The New York Times Magazine*, April 28, 1985.

perience. They were an isolation, but they afforded the safety of not being home, of not exposing oneself to the attention, the hostility, the betrayal of one's own people.

GO: The most damaging effect of the wartime internment on Japanese was the fear and sense of shame it instilled. What the internment taught Japanese Americans is not only that there is danger in being different, but also that there is safety in resembling the majority. One young man after Pearl Harbor had an eye operation in an attempt to disguise his race. It didn't fool the authorities, of course, because for Asians and other people of color there are limits to how much we can physically resemble the majority. That is a problem because it makes us less free to explore and express our cultural roots and affinities—those facets of our character and personality that give us our individuality and identity. Our racial difference can be a prison, if the fear and shame of being different outwardly causes us to deny our inward differences.

Thanks to the civil rights movement racial differences are no longer the absolute bar to social-economic success they once were. Asian Americans in particular have made great strides in overcoming racial barriers and in some quarters we have been recognized for our success as a "model minority." The phrase is one that touches a complex, often contradictory, set of reactions among Asian Americans. As a Japanese American I feel humiliated by the notion that I am one of the white majority's model minority because I sense that our model behavior is motivated largely by fear. The Japanese American "nice guy" persona is a culturally determined one, to be sure, but traced back to its Japanese roots, it is frequently the posture a socially inferior individual assumes towards a superior. It is a progression and transformation of our physical imprisonment to a general state of cultural and spiritual bondage.

I began my professional career nearly forty years ago as a newspaper reporter. The newspaper profession was a white profession, but it suited me because a reporter is an observer of events, not a participant. My profession could accommodate my sense of alienation, indeed give it a protective covering. A crisis in my life came in 1980 when I accepted the position of press secretary to the governor of Maryland—a prominent and highly visible insider position, a member of the Governor's "senior staff." There should have been some attenuation of the sense of being an outsider, but instead it grew stronger. Being so prominently an insider intensified my feeling of isolation instead of ameliorating it and after two years I resigned my position.

It was at that point that I began seriously to examine my past. For some years I had been working on a novel about the Japanese American experience. As an early indication of how strongly I was repressing my wartime experience, the book as originally conceived would have avoided the camp experience altogether. My rationalization was that there had already been enough written about the camps and there was more to the Japanese American experience than the internment. I did not want our imprisonment to be, so to speak, our claim to fame. When I resumed work on the novel, however, I began to experience sudden and unexpected emotional breakdowns. At one point I found myself weeping when I had a character in the novel say to himself, "I am Japanese." As I continued to be ambushed in this manner I began to understand that I was tapping some deep emotional well, and that it had been placed there by my wartime experience. I could not avoid the camp experience any longer; it was something I had to confront. So I dropped the novel, and wrote instead an autobiography that focused on the internment. It was something I had to do to get on with my life. It was also something I had to do for my children, who in some mysterious way had inherited the shame and fear of an imprisonment that occurred decades before their birth.

EO: The legacy of the internment has been a powerful one for me, and has, in many ways, shaped the course of my life and my work. The need to investigate, to write, to break silences, to dig deeply and insistently into the hidden nature of truth, the understanding that this work is necessary to save your life: these are things I inherited from my father. From my mother, a Ph.D. (herself the daughter of a Ph.D.), I learned to value the importance of education. From my father, with his curiosity about the world, his difficult and lifelong journey of self-exploration, I learned to be an intellectual.

In her film *History and Memory*, filmmaker Rea Tajiri says about the internment camp in Poston: "There was this place that they knew about. I had never been there, yet I have a memory for it."[19] I too, have felt haunted by memories of a place I have never been, and I needed to understand where these images, this knowledge, this awareness came from.

For my father's 67th birthday I sent him a box of stones that I had purchased from the Japanese American National Museum gift shop in Los Angeles. They are called "mystery stones," and they are replicas of stones that were unearthed from the site of the internment camp in Heart Mountain, Wyoming. After the internees left, a farmer discovered a 50-gallon oil drum that had been filled with small, polished stones and buried. Each stone was carefully painted with a Chinese character. After many years, the stones were taken to the Japanese American National Museum. No one has been able to discover the creators or the significance of these stones. Perhaps they were the words of a Buddhist chant, perhaps some kind of poetry, perhaps another improvised ritual. They remain one of the buried mysteries of the internment. I do not know the real, the "authentic" origin of these stones, but I do know that they bear the words "kaeru" (to return), "tomo" (go together), "yume" (dream), "chikara" (strength) and "ten" (heaven). As Eric Liu has written in his book *The Accidental Asian*, "What matters, after a while, is not the memory of shared experience so much as the shared experience of memory."[20] This journey—this paper, this trip—taken together, is meant as a kind of excavation of memory, not of an objective, intact past, but of an abiding legacy, the ways in which the unspoken experiences of the past, transmitted down through family lines, reassert themselves insistently in the present.

GO: I will conclude my part of this paper with a few observations concerning our visit this week to the site of my internment. My daughter will have thoughts of her own, this having been her first

---

[19] Tajiri, Rea, 1992. *History and Memory: For Akiko and Takashige*. Women Make Movies.

[20] Liu, Eric, *The Accidental Asian: Notes of a Native Speaker* (New York: Vintage Books, 1998): 9-10.

visit. I have been there twice before, and I have signed my wife and all of my children and their spouses for the tour tomorrow. My wife, Sabine, went with me on the first return visit in 1982, and it was at her suggestion the other visits have taken place and will take place tomorrow. She has always understood better than I the profound and lasting impact the internment has had on my life. It has taken me decades to acknowledge something that should have been obvious from the start. But for me, as it was for others of my generation, the experience was something not to be remembered, not to be discussed, and, most important of all, not to be passed on to my children.

I understand today that to withhold memories and feelings stemming from the internment is to withhold a big part of myself, and to withhold something that in a circuitous way has become a part of their lives as well. So it is important for them to see this piece of desert landscape, even if it is now surrounded by groves of olive and citrus trees, by fields of watermelon, alfalfa, barley and oats. None of this was there sixty years ago. It was still a desert wilderness as far as one could see.

What my family will see tomorrow will be different in a fundamental way from what I experienced as a child. They will need to use their imagination to understand two quite opposite feelings that my very first encounter with this landscape produced in me: first, the terror of isolation in this desolate land where we could be forgotten and left to die. And two, what eventually became a comfort and a feeling of safety in a desert vastness far removed from civilization. That the very remoteness of this wild and untamed land could hold such paradoxical meanings can perhaps be seen as a metaphor for the complex and often paradoxical feelings I have had most of my life living in working in America. That insight grows stronger with each visit to the camp site.

EO: May 25, 11:00 a.m. I have finally made it to Gila, the site of so much of my family's history. We have climbed to the top of the tallest butte and are looking across the valley of sagebrush, mesquite and saguaro, over to the newly planted farmland that interrupts the desert and stretches to the mountains. My first thought is that it's so much smaller than I remember. I have the experience that one has as an adult when one visits an old school, house, or neighborhood from childhood. Everything seems so much smaller. How strange that I am experiencing this place, where I have never been, as smaller than my memory. But for me it has always been a place in which children live and which lives in childhood. I have inherited my father's childhood memories—my own childhood was peopled with them—and this place is resonant with the magic, the fragility and the ordinariness of childhood.

It feels good to be here. We began our journey responsibly and correctly, armed with sunscreen and bottled water. From his earlier research, my father had learned that, while the Gila River Indian Reservation was not open to the public, one could apply for a permit, and people who had been interned in the camps on the land were allowed to visit. This was done as a favor to the Japanese American Citizens League, to protect the site from too much tourism, and to preserve it for the former residents and their families. When we got to the Gila River Indian Center, however, we were met with a bureaucratic stonewall. The woman we asked told us that the only way that we could go would be to call "Elaine" (the name scribbled on a post-it on the phone book) from a pay phone, go to the appropriate office and apply for a permit. No, she would not tell us where the site was. Yes, we would be "picked up and taken in" if we were caught without a permit on the land. We called the number we were given and, of course, there was no one in the office. We needed the help of the office to find the site, but, suddenly, I couldn't stand the thought of waiting for them. I was damned if I was going to start this journey as a passive supplicant, meekly waiting outside of office doors, chasing a paper trail of forms and messages. Everything that I had been thinking, writing about and reading from my father rose up and refused to do it. No more model minority. No more waiting for permission.

We were, of course, aware of the irony of setting the tribal administration as our antagonists. The fact that Gila River and many of the camps were built on reservations, established through the forcible removal and relocation of Native Americans from their ancestral lands, is another example of the contiguous, overlapping, and incommensurable treatment of minority groups by the U.S. government. In the last days of the war, as Japanese American families were starting to leave the camp (my father and his family had been relocated to a camp in Poston), my father remembers families of Hopi Indians beginning to settle into the tar-papered barracks that were being abandoned by the Japanese families.[21] We knew that we were on Indian land, and that our access to the site, considered sacred by the Gila River Indian Community, was a gift granted to the former internees. But on that day, faced with the prospect of an indefinite delay, we suddenly found that our normally reserved and respectful stance could no longer hold. The buildup to this visit had made it impossible for us to wait for the correct form.

We eventually found the spot, with the help of some friendly farmers. We never really expected to be "picked up" by the tribal police, but we celebrated with jokes. A crop duster barreling towards us became a fighter plane, machine guns aimed at our car to take us down. Small white crosses by the side of the road became memorials for other trespassers who had been caught without their permits. I more than halfway wished that we would get arrested. "Free the Gila Two!" my father shouted.

It was a funny but very moving experience: we were claiming something as our own—an action, a history, a place. As we drove through more and more fields and orchards that had not been there before, my father remarked, "Look what they've done to my desert. Those goddamn farmers!" I had never heard him speak of it as belonging to him. It was something that happened to you, not something that you could own. I didn't know what I had expected to find, but I had thought about camp as an overwhelming force of history, a

---

[21] About this time, my father writes: "When the war ended, Poston gradually began to empty. In the block next to ours a family of Hopi Indians moved into one of the barracks. . . The grandfather of the family liked to talk to us and he told us how the white man had taken their land away. One day, he said, there would be a great Indian uprising and they would take all the land back. Later, other Indian families began to move into the camp and sometimes late at night you could hear an Indian brave shouting what might have been a war chant at the top of his lungs. It seems eerie when I think back on our final days in Poston, on a community of imprisoned Japanese beginning to scatter, the barracks taking on a look of deterioration as the desert reasserted its claim, and the Hopi Indians, the true owners of the land, gathering slowly, prophesying war." *Hiroshi* pp. 75-6.

thing that had to be struggled against and feared. What I found was that it was a gift that my father could give me, a simple day spent alone together, a small plot of land with rusty nails, concrete slabs of foundation and slate green sage plants.

My father gives me a stick of wood with which to test the brush for snakes (Snakes?!!! That wasn't part of the fantasy. I rehearse what I would do if either of us is bitten: cut the wound, suck out the poison, that's all I remember) and I follow him up the path he took hundreds of times in childhood to the top of a tall butte. At the top he shows me the stone where he used to sit, and where his older brother, Goro, explained to him the reason that people in China aren't upside down despite being on the other side of the earth. He said that what we experience as "down" is always the direction of the gravitational force. No matter where we are on the globe, the earth's center exerts its pull on us and creates for us a sense of direction, of up and down. Sitting there I think, how funny that my father and I, both notorious amongst our family and friends for our complete and utter lack of geographical direction, should have found our way so clearly to this very spot. I think that we create our own knowledge and direction in this life, based on the gravitational pull of history, of family, of place. I think about my family, I look to the mountains and to the horizon, and I draw my compass points.

A (YONSEI) EDITOR'S NOTE:
SEEING OURSELVES ACROSS GENERATIONAL LINES

ANA IWATAKI

In 1988, when Gene Oishi's memoir was originally published by the Charles E. Tuttle Company, the camps had been closed for more than forty years. This was also the year that the Redress Movement achieved its greatest victory, with the Civil Liberties Act of 1988 granting $20,000 in reparations for each camp survivor, as well as a presidential apology.

I was born in 1989, long after the camps, a year after redress and reparations. What was to Oishi a childhood trauma has been passed down to me as an inherited trauma. I was raised in the West Coast Japanese American community, where incarceration is a foundational moment become foundational narrative. As I've navigated my life, I've had no choice but to grapple with camp and its afterlives. This is especially true because camp stories, which continue to shape Japanese American identity, politics, and culture, have been repeated, manipulated, and updated across various genres, forms, and platforms.

Oishi's book is, for me, an inheritance in multiple ways. Having been invited to take part as an editor in helping to present this story that began well before my birth, I've tried to discern what it means for me, a Yonsei (fourth-generation JA), to be creative and commemorative in this particular moment. Above all I've had to consider how to be an effective conduit between generations. What are my responsibilities both towards Oishi and towards those who will come after me?

My hope is that Kaya Press's revised edition of *In Search of Hiroshi* provides additional context to the particularities of Oishi's Nisei story by including evidence of is intergenerational reverberations. Introduced by new writing by Oishi and concluded by a joint paper presented by Oishi and his daughter Eve Oishi at an academic conference, this project provides an opportunity to consider the changing nature of the memory of incarceration across lifespans and generations. The scholarly and political frameworks at our disposal today have transformed our understanding of the camp experience.

Before reading *In Search of Hiroshi*, I thought I knew Oishi's story. I was raised in what felt at times like an over-saturation of camp narratives, so much so that I was convinced I could analyze those experiences better than those who lived through them. The "camp story" felt to me like a genre whose broad strokes I could fill in myself. But Oishi's memoir is the record of an individual working through decades of trauma: as such it can't be reduced to broad strokes.

This became clearer to me the more I worked and talked with Oishi. For him, the possibility of working with a Yonsei editor is certainly one obvious change from 1988, when the Tuttle Company, which was founded by an American stationed in Japan during the war, was one of the few publishing options for Japanese American writers.

Some conversations revealed the assumptions I have from being raised in the bosom of the West Coast Asian American Movement. I was very surprised that he had never heard of the Day of Remembrance, the annual commemoration of the signing of Executive Order 9066, which originated in the 1970s as part of the organizing for redress and reparations. It has since become a mainstream part of JA culture, observed by most individuals and organizations regardless of their politics. It was in moments like this that I began to have a more visceral understanding of what it meant for Oishi to attempt to escape his racial identity for so long.

Choosing to live in Europe and on the East Coast, he removed himself almost completely from the JA community in his adult life. He noted that over the decades almost none of the reader responses to his articles or books have been from JAs. For Oishi, writing about and through trauma has often been a truly solitary process.

Other times, I felt the connection of our cultural identity more than our generational or geographic divide. Speaking to Oishi one day about the model minority myth led to a conversation about the many ways JA complexity is flattened, including within the community itself. I have found that many JAs feel alienated by the simplified narratives of who we are. What might it mean to recognize self-alienation as a shared cultural inheritance? And how can intergenerational conversation help to overcome that alienation?

Oishi began to experience the profound impact of connecting to the Sansei generation in the 1980s, when he travelled the country interviewing JAs for the assignment that would become "The Anxiety of Being Japanese-American." Breaking his self-imposed isolation and "[s]eeing [his] own nisei generation from across generational lines" was particularly transformative, even when it came in the form of blunt criticism. We laughed as I reassured him that the Sansei were now receiving their own fair share from my generation as well. Yonsei and even Gosei (fifth-generation) scholars and activists are contesting and rewriting the meaning of not only camp but other "primal moments" such as redress and reparations. Japanese American identity is being considered through a range of new political and personal perspectives, aided by frameworks that take into consideration questions of diaspora and settler colonialism.

But even as a new generation of writers and scholars strive to deepen and broader our understanding of the "camp story," it also seems important to try to read between the fault lines that continue to exist between the generations. Oishi touched on this as well:

"The complaint I've heard from Sansei is that my parents just won't talk about it. And they're upset about that. Well, I did want to talk about it, but not to my children so much, but to the public in general being a journalist...."

Eve Oishi's new introduction to their joint paper describes a different dynamic of familial disclosure, calling themselves "lucky to have a father who shared many details of his childhood, even if the sharing was part of a painful process of self-discovery that we were witness to." Oishi's search engendered their own, with scholarship born from "an attempt to trace the things that I knew and felt back to events from before I was born."

Oishi's memoir is thus an occasion to reflect on not only the impact of incarceration, but also the shifting nature of alienation across and between generations. For Oishi, writing was a long, lonely search for internal resolution. And at the same time, his story informs Eve Oishi's, mine, and so many others in ways he couldn't anticipate. At one point he commented to me that having lived through it, he has little appetite for analyzing incarceration's aftermath. Its meaning for and impact on younger generations, even his own children, is not his story to tell. He told me, "That's for you to write."

Still, as the living memory of camps fades, it seems ever more vital to not let our contemporary readings—our post-memories—supersede completely those that came before. The evolving nature of "our" narrative and "our" identity is made and made singular in Oishi's search. Over the course of a long life, the texture and transformations of silence and self-disclosure are lived and written differently. The richness of our bodies of literature, scholarship, political organizing, and the identities and communities they engender, are indebted to these kinds of records. For me, and for those who come after me, *In Search of Hiroshi* can be at turns a gift from an elder, to be treated with reverence, and an invitation to do with it what we will.

AUTHOR

GENE OISHI, former Washington and foreign correspondent for *The Baltimore Sun*, has also written articles on the Japanese American experience for *The New York Times Magazine*, *The Washington Post*, *Newsweek*, and *West Magazine*. His memoir, *In Search of Hiroshi*, was published in 1988. Now retired, he lives in Baltimore, Maryland with his wife Sabine.

CONTRIBUTORS

EVE OISHI is Associate Professor of Cultural Studies at Claremont Graduate University specializing in Asian American media and gender studies.

ANA IWATAKI is a cultural historian, writer, and curator from and based in Los Angeles.